Are You Serious About Love?

Is there a way to *really* know if someone is right for you?

According to Dr. Kay Kuzma, YES! In the pages of this book, you'll learn how to evaluate your present—or future—relationships. And you'll find plenty of down-to-earth guidance for dating and love, including

- ❤ What to look for—and watch out for—in a potential date

- ❤ How to understand the difference between romantic illusion and true love

- ❤ How to break up and remain friends

- ❤ What physical involvement means to a relationship

- ❤ How to be a great mate

- ❤ Topics to discuss before considering marriage

- ❤ How to make your dreams come true

Whether you're dating someone or just looking forward to meeting "the right one," this book will help you understand the serious side of love.

When You're SERIOUS About LOVE

DR. KAY KUZMA

Here's Life Publishers

First Printing, July 1992

Published by
HERE'S LIFE PUBLISHERS, INC.
P. O. Box 1576
San Bernardino, CA 92402

Cover design by David Marty Design

Library of Congress Cataloging-in-Publication Data
Kuzma, Kay.
    When you're serious about love : straight talk to single adults / Kay Kuzma.
        p.   cm.
    ISBN 0-89840-355-3
    1. Man-woman relationships—United States. 2. Dating (Social customs).
3. Mate selection—United States. I. Title.
HQ801.Z89 1992
646.7'7—dc20   92-15061
                                            CIP

Upon the release of each new book, Here's Life Publishers sponsors the planting of a tree through Global ReLeaf ™, a program of the American Forestry Association.

Unless indicated otherwise Scripture quotations are from *The Holy Bible: New King James Version*, © 1982 by Thomas Nelson, Inc., Nashville, Tennessee. Scripture quotations designated KJV are from the *King James Version*. Scripture quotations designated NASB are from *The New American Standard Bible*, © The Lockman Foundation 1960, 1962, 1963, 1968, 1971, 1972, 1975, 1977. Scripture quotations designated NIV are from *The Holy Bible: New International Version*, © 1973, 1978, 1984 by the International Bible Society. Published by Zondervan Bible Publishers, Grand Rapids, Michigan. Scripture quotations designated TLB are from *The Living Bible*, © 1971 by Tyndale House Publishers, Wheaton, Illinois.

For More Information, Write:
    L.I.F.E.—P.O. Box A399, Sydney South 2000, Australia
    Campus Crusade for Christ of Canada—Box 300, Vancouver, B.C., V6C 2X3, Canada
    Campus Crusade for Christ—Pearl Assurance House, 4 Temple Row, Birmingham, B2 5HG, England
    Lay Institute for Evangelism—P.O. Box 8786, Auckland 3, New Zealand
    Campus Crusade for Christ—P.O. Box 240, Raffles City Post Office, Singapore 9117
    Great Commission Movement of Nigeria—P.O. Box 500, Jos, Plateau State Nigeria, West Africa
    Campus Crusade for Christ International—100 Sunport Lane, Orlando, FL 32809, U.S.A.

Dedicated to my children,

Kimberly and her husband
Kari and her special friend
Kevin and his surfboard

May you always remember that . . .
"Through wisdom a house is built,
And by understanding it is established;
By knowledge the rooms are filled
With all precious and pleasant riches."
Proverbs 24:3,4

Contents

♥   ♥

Introduction

Are you anticipating making an investment in marriage sometime soon? Marriage isn't like the stock market—you don't pick up a good-looking marriage partner and hold on to it as long as it proves to be a good investment and then dump it for another when it starts to slump. Marriage is an investment for life.

You owe it to yourself to find out what it takes to be happy and fulfilled in a lifetime commitment. Do you have the information you need to choose a marriage partner wisely?

You're mature enough to realize that love and marriage aren't necessarily forever. You've watched your friends fall in love, marry and divorce. Others are struggling to hold things together, and many are merely existing as married singles. You want something better. Not only do you want to avoid the devastating agony of rejection and divorce, but you also want to experience all that God intended marital love to be.

This book is for those who are serious about love. It is for you who have gone through the teenage turmoil of falling in and out of puppy love and are now seriously searching for a lifetime marriage partner.

Walk as rationally as possible through the dating process. Give yourself time to determine whether you are courting the right mate. There is nothing more

9

bankrupting than making a long-term investment in what turns out to be a short-term interest.

Don't give up your idealism. It is possible to have your dreams come true. In spite of difficult days, you can experience a sustaining sense of intimate, unconditional love in your marriage. But don't kid yourself—it won't happen by chance.

Whether you find the happiness you're looking for depends a great deal on two factors: choosing the right mate and being the right mate for the person you choose. A little advice: Choose wisely. Love is not enough to keep a marriage together.

If you are serious about love, read this book with your loved one. Make a promise to yourself and to each other to evaluate the risk factors for alienation and divorce. Work out major and minor problems in your relationship *before* you marry.

Marriage is a commitment for life. Live before marriage so you can experience complete life and love after you say "I do." That's what this book is all about.

Kay Kuzma

♥ 1 ♥

What Do You Want Out of Marriage?

A bishop was administering confirmation to a group of young people and asked a nervous child, "How does the catechism define matrimony?"

The child hesitated for a moment and then said, "It is a state of terrible torment, which those who are compelled to enter undergo for a time to fit them for the better world."

"No, no," interrupted the parish priest. "You're mixed up with the definition of purgatory!"

"Let it be," smiled the bishop. "How do two priests like you and I know that the child is not right?"

Every bride and groom says "I do" with the expectation that *their* marriage is going to be different. They believe their union will bring true fulfillment and intimacy. A young couple would never walk down the aisle if they knew they were entering a state of "purgatory." People get married because they dream of living happily ever after. They want heaven on earth—not hell!

But so few reach the ideal. Why is that? Is there something you can do to make sure your marriage will be everything you are hoping it will be?

Choosing a Marriage Partner

Marriage is a pivotal point. In one way or another, everything beyond it will be affected by the one you choose as your mate. *Choosing a marriage partner who will stand the test of time is the most important decision you will ever have to make.* Yet many people are more serious about checking out the car they want to buy than the person they want to marry. Can you imagine buying a car on feelings alone?

If you want to avoid marital misery, you have to have a goal above and beyond merely finding the person who turns you on. And it's probably not wise to get married just because you've found someone who meets your needs. You must consider every aspect of the other person's life in relationship to your own.

Marriage is a lifelong commitment to a one-flesh relationship, regardless of personality, handicaps, temperament, money, looks or health. This commitment shouldn't be hard to keep. *It shouldn't be work!* To love your mate as yourself is meant to be the most natural response of your being.

It takes a great deal of effort to have a good marriage, but it doesn't have to be a chore. If you have a job just for that paycheck, that's work. But if your job is something you would do regardless of the pay, you can give it everything you've got and it doesn't seem like work at all. Every successful marriage takes effort, but if you marry the "right" mate for you and you choose to be the right mate for the person you marry, you'll find satisfaction is easier to obtain.

I believe many marriages end up in a "terrible state of torment" because people too quickly follow their feelings. They make poor choices in the person they go steady with, and then hope their beloved will magically change, become their ideal mate and bring them lasting fulfillment. Let me tell you, that never happens.

Avoiding the Less-Than-Ideal Marriage

Before you can choose a mate, you have to decide what you want out of marriage. You need to know where you're going in order to determine how to get there.

Most people want romance, intimacy, a sense of fulfillment and companionship in a marriage. They want an equal partnership—not a union where one dominates the other. The ideal marriage is two people continuing to grow in love, understanding and unity. They are totally committed to meeting each other's needs regardless of health, wealth or whether the cap gets put on the toothpaste. That's marital bliss.

Most newlyweds start out expecting that theirs will be the ideal marriage, but few retain this expectation past the first five years. The ideal is only possible when the couple commits to and actively works on keeping their marriage vital.

Many marriages simply die after the first few years. The divorce statistics verify this fact. And what happens to the rest? They may survive, but too often they become something less than the ideal. Usually these marriages fall into one of the following categories: a marriage of convenience, a devitalized marriage, a dominant/submissive marriage or a conflict-filled marriage.

Let's peek at these less-than-ideal marriages. If you don't like what you see and want to avoid them, the rest of this book will guide you through your dating and courtship period so your marriage can be everything you want it to be. If you date wisely, you will have the best possible chance of experiencing a dynamic marriage where both partners are committed to growing together in a meaningful, lifelong relationship.

The Convenient Marriage

In a marriage of convenience, the partners need each other to pay the bills and take care of the kids, to entertain and share the driving on vacation. But as far as the day-to-day routine, there is very little, if any, pizzazz in their relationship. They might consider getting a divorce, but for the time being it's just convenient for the kids and each other to stick it out, even though marital satisfaction is low.

Jerry and Trish live in a convenient marriage relationship. Jerry is a physician with a life of his own. He needs a wife to take care of things on the home front, and Trish is comfortable to have around. If something ever happened to her, he admits he would get married again.

"Being married solves a lot of problems," he says. "You have someone to cook meals, do the shopping, entertain guests, and someone to escort to social functions."

And how does Trish feel about her marriage?

"Well," she says, "it's certainly not the Romeo and Juliet romance I used to fantasize about when I was a kid. I knew my parents had a marriage of convenience—they would have never survived out on the farm without each other—but I never thought my marriage was going to turn out like this.

"It's a stable marriage, though, so I'm a lot better off than many of my friends. I know Jerry needs me to keep things up around the house, but he has his own career and I have mine. I've just recently become the chairman of the United Way campaign in our district and find myself working almost as hard as Jerry. I have my own friends and Jerry has his.

"At night it's nice to know there is someone around. It would be terribly lonely living alone now that the kids have left the nest."

This is a typical marriage of convenience. It isn't a bad marriage; it's just not the type most young lovers look forward to.

What causes a marriage to sift down to this living arrangement? It may be that the couple did not share the same ideal of what type of marriage they wanted. Or their ideas of marriage may have changed with the reality of daily responsibilities and busy schedules. They may not have had the communication skills necessary to discuss what was happening to their relationship or the commitment to turn it around. Similar interests which serve to pull a couple together might have been missing. Without these vital ingredients, it's easy for a dynamic honeymoon to disintegrate into a marriage of convenience.

The Devitalized Marriage

The devitalized marriage starts out with high expectations and a keen sense of romance, but early in the marriage something happens. The couple forgets to continue those early attentions. They may have gotten married in the passion stage of their relationship and exchanged vows before they learned to communicate their needs. They didn't realize the importance of continuing to court each other after the intense feelings of desire mellowed to a stable state of true love. And now they wonder, "Why did we get married?"

More women than men categorize their marriages as devitalized, probably because women tend to entertain romantic fantasies and may not be as fulfilled in their careers as men. These women usually get married with the idea that their Prince Charming will continue to sweep them off their feet as he did during their courtship. Unfortunately, many Prince Charmings tend to perform valiantly only when there is a prize to be won. Once the wedding and honeymoon are over, they move on to other conquests—not women, necessarily, but educational pursuits, career advancements, various leisure-time activities or the stock market. These men love their wives, but they don't really see the value of spending lots of time together, especially if they have different interests and life objectives.

As men near the mid-life crisis years (forty to fifty-five), some wake up to the fact that their marriage is no longer very exciting. Now, having achieved educational, career, athletic and financial objectives, too many men think their lack of fulfillment stems from having married the wrong woman.

Here is what Robin said about her devitalized marriage: "Richard was a real Romeo during our courtship. Can you imagine, he even hired a couple of his friends to play their guitars and sing outside my dorm window on my birthday. I was really surprised when he asked me for that first date because he ran around with an entirely different crowd than I. They were the partying type and enjoyed going to the beach or playing tennis on the weekends rather than attending church and giving some of their time to help others. But when I got to know Richard, I liked him. Though we didn't have too much in common, he added a sparkle to my life.

"If you had known Richard back in college, you wouldn't believe the change in him now. He's all work and no play, and our marriage has become dull—really dull. With three preschoolers, I have my hands full. On the weekends he often asks me to play tennis with him, but I don't enjoy the game that much and hate to make a fool of myself. Sometimes he suggests going to the beach, but it's a lot of trouble to take three preschoolers anywhere. I'm afraid I'd rather stay home with a good book.

"I know I've grown a little shabby since I'm home all the time, but if Richard would only bring me a rose, or call me passionately on the phone as he used to do, I'd feel more like going the extra mile to make myself more attractive. As it is now, I doubt if he'd even notice."

Would you like to hear how things are from Richard's perspective?

"Robin was one of the most admired women on campus. She was a school leader and highly involved in church programs. That's why I was so surprised she accepted a date with me when I first asked her. I knew I was going to have to do something different to get her attention. I guess I fell for her because I knew I could get almost any girl on campus, but Robin didn't seem to be interested in me. She was a challenge, and I liked that.

"It wasn't long before we got married, and then everything seemed to change. I was always suggesting we go places and do things, and she preferred to stay home. Reading some religious book was not my idea of a good time, so before long we had fallen into a pattern of each doing our own thing.

"I never expected marriage to be this way. I dreamed of my wife greeting me at the door and showering me with kisses when I got home after a hard day at work. I dreamed of us walking on the beach hand-in-hand, or playing a good game of tennis and later relaxing in the spa. But it's like pulling hair to get Robin to do anything with me. That's why I've sort of given up.

"I guess we are two different people, with different

expectations and different needs. Marriage certainly isn't what I thought it was going to be."

Both Robin and Richard realize that they have a devitalized marriage, but each seems powerless to make changes. If they had taken more time during their courtship to get deeply acquainted with each other, if they had realized how different their interests were, I wonder if they would have gotten married.

The Dominant/Submissive Marriage

We laugh about the husband being the head of the family and the wife being the neck that turns the head. We make fun of the hen-pecked husband. We tell jokes about the day in heaven when they asked all the men to line up behind two signs: one read, "Supreme head of the family," and the other, "Attempted head of the family."

All the men lined up in front of the "Attempted head" sign except one small man. The others were shocked. How could this man be so bold as to stand in front of that "Supreme head of the family" sign? He must have a tremendous strength of character underneath his slight, wimpish frame. Finally, one of the men got up nerve to go over to the man and ask him why he was standing in the "Supreme head" line. "Oh," replied the man, "my wife told me to stand here."

While it's fairly plain to see that a dominant wife is not good in a marriage, what about a dominant husband?

Elly had been married to Al for twelve years. The children were now in school and she had a great desire to go back and finish her education. But Al refused.

Char read every marriage book that came along and took every seminar. Her greatest desire was to be the best wife and mother in the world. She tried to share her findings with Bill, but he wouldn't listen. "That newfangled psychology will just get you into trouble," was his response. Char began to feel that she was always the one who was molding to fit the needs of Bill. And Bill had no interest in changing.

Dan kept a tight accounting of the finances, giving Bonnie a weekly allowance for food and supplies. At the end of the week Bonnie had to account for every penny. She couldn't even get herself a candy bar without reporting to Dan.

Whenever the kids asked her for favors, Missy would automatically say, "Ask your father." Ted was the final authority in everything. Missy was always saying to her friends, "I wanted to call you last night, but Ted said it was too late," or "I would love to attend your weekly Bible study, but Ted thinks I spend too much time away from the house as it is," or "I love chocolate, but Ted won't let me eat it."

Keith didn't want to be the supreme head of the family, but after Lynn attended a seminar on how to be a good Christian wife, she deferred all the household decisions to him. "Honey, I would like to hang a picture in the living room, but I want to make sure you approve." "Lacey is feeling a little sick today. Do you think I should keep her home?" "Is it okay if I buy some material to make myself a dress? Should I get blue or red?" "Do you want to sign Jeff's report card, or should I?" Before marriage Lynn seemed quite capable of making good decisions on her own—that's why Keith married her. Now her submissiveness was driving him up a wall.

Many Christian young people have been conditioned to think that husbands should be the head of the family, but no one would want to find themselves in any of those situations. The ideal is to recognize God as the head of the family, and side-by-side the husband

and wife lead in the family's daily affairs in areas where each is most competent.

Only when conflict arises is it important to have an established pattern of authority as is suggested in Ephesians 5:21-28. Notice the first instruction is that both should submit to each other. However, when you come to an irreconcilable difference, somebody has to submit. God instructed that rather than fight over that as well, wives should submit.

The biblical instruction makes good sense, but God did not create Adam to be Eve's superior. He created Adam and Eve to be equal partners in a lifelong commitment to each other. And even today, when it comes down to practical daily living and marriage satisfaction, most lovers want an egalitarian marriage.

The Conflict-Filled Marriage

A conflict-dominated marriage occurs when each partner is convinced of his or her infallibility and becomes rigid and defensive. Neither one sees a need to learn the art of negotiation. Why compromise when your opinion is right?

Before marriage, because each is trying so hard to please the other, it is sometimes difficult to determine just how prone a couple might be to experience a conflict-filled marriage someday. Ideally, this wanting-to-please-each-other behavior should continue throughout marriage, but it seldom does. After marriage, each feels more free to express an opinion without regard for how it might make the other person feel. In a good marriage, where each respects the other, the free expression of personal opinions is healthy. But where there isn't much respect, too often the conflict results in hostility. When this happens, the time the couple could spend enjoying each other is eaten away in senseless battles.

Why don't these couples get a divorce? As one woman said, "If we get a divorce, who would we have to argue with?" One husband commented, "I would never let myself become involved in this type of arguing in any other relationship, but it just seems the thing to do with my wife."

God designed the marriage institution to provide a safe climate for growth and change. Marriage is meant to be an ideal relationship where each partner is nurtured and supported in such a way as to increase individual and joint potential. The effect of living in a conflict-filled marriage is exactly the opposite: It stifles growth and improvement. In addition, hostile words dishonor God (Matthew 5:21,22). As long as the devil can keep a couple arguing, their marriage will be a "state of terrible torment," regardless of whether or not they consider divorce.

How can you determine if your relationship is heading toward a conflict-filled marriage? Watch for signs of nagging, bossiness or any other behavior you find irritating. It's possible to be so infatuated that you overlook negative behavior patterns or think that these will be overcome with love. Unfortunately, after marriage, when the relationship is secure and the realization begins to dawn that this undesirable behavior is increasing instead of decreasing, the previously docile partner is likely to begin standing up for his or her rights. The result? More conflict.

Danielle was a born leader. She was outgoing, talkative, decisive and quick to point out what needed to be done in order to solve a problem. She respected people who were experts in their fields and often criticized those who weren't. She married Travis. He thought carefully before speaking, took his time to get things done and would never think of pushing others or himself. He may have appeared on the outside to be fairly compliant because of his quiet ways, but he had a strong mind of his own.

Things went well until the faucet started leaking and the house needed painting. "Travis, do you know how many gallons of water we are wasting with that leaky faucet?" Danielle asked. "It's got to be fixed this weekend."

But Travis was in the middle of a book and read the weekend away.

"Travis, I can't stand this peeling paint," Danielle complained. "Either you get this house scraped and painted, or I'll use our vacation money and have a professional painter do it."

Travis calmly stated, "I'll do it." And he was going to, but he wasn't about to miss a finance seminar that was going on that week. Two months later the faucet still leaked and the house paint was still peeling.

Danielle grew more disturbed. Why couldn't Travis be more like her father who was interested in keeping things in good repair around the home? Travis was so clumsy when it came to practical things like fixing the toaster or putting up wallpaper. (She hadn't noticed this before marriage.) The more she criticized him, the more her respect for him dropped—and the more biting her tongue became.

For seven years Travis calmly took this abuse, and then one day he stood up to her. His pent-up hostility caused him to say hurtful, mean things in front of the children. He had lost respect for his wife and treated her accordingly.

Chances are Danielle and Travis never truly respected each other in the first place. If you respect another person you will not nag or boss, even if your natural self feels like it. You will check your words and speak with respect.

If Danielle and Travis hadn't rushed into marriage (because summer was a convenient time to get married), these obnoxious, conflict-causing traits would have probably surfaced before their wedding date. They could have made a more informed choice.

If you want to avoid a conflict-filled marriage, give yourselves the time you need to analyze carefully every noticeable trait about each other. Ask yourself, "Can I learn to love and respect that trait?" Take time to discuss the behavior that bothers you. There's a lot more motivation for changing traits before marriage than after! For those traits where change is highly unlikely, discuss how these might affect your marriage. While it's impossible to anticipate everything that might surface in your marriage, the more potential problems you recognize and deal with before the wedding date, the fewer the heartbreaking surprises afterward.

So, the question remains, what do you want out of marriage? If you want a dynamic marriage with your love for each other growing stronger and more intimate each passing year, then it becomes absolutely essential that throughout your courtship you continually assess whether you are dating the right mate—and whether you are the right mate for the person you're dating.

❤ ❤ ❤

Something to Think About . . .

What do you want out of marriage? Take some time to write down your answer. If you are seriously dating someone, discuss your expectations of marriage with each other. In what ways do you agree? How do you disagree? Are your disagreements signaling potential problem areas?

♥ 2 ♥

Date the Right Mate or Beware of Your Fate

It's easy to fall in love. Most people fall in love many times before they are really serious about love—often with individuals who would make very poor marriage partners. Obviously you won't marry everyone you fall in love with, but the chances are quite high that you will promise to love, honor and obey someone you will date in the next few years.

Too many people say, "I do," in the heat of romance, only to discover that hot summer love isn't necessarily rational. *It is possible to be madly in love with the wrong person. And being in love is not reason enough to marry.* Marriages based on love alone may make it through the fall of a relationship as passion begins to cool, but when love settles down for a long winter's night—and rationality returns—too many discover that they have made a long-term investment in a short-term interest.

Have you ever heard someone say after the first date or two, "I could never fall in love with him!" or "She's not my type, but there's nobody else to date right now." Too often these same individuals are sending out wedding invitations six months later.

Beware! No matter what you may tell yourself,

given the right conditions you can fall in love with almost anyone. And it all starts out with that first date. That's why it is very important to assess the person you continue to date to make sure he or she has the characteristics you want in a mate.

There are actually two types of dating, but the line between them is not always easy to distinguish. *Friendship dating* is when you are just interested in making new friends. You do things in groups and you have little desire to continue dating the same individual. *Serious dating* is where you desire to continue the dating relationship. Whether you admit it or not, you are searching for someone whom you'd like to marry. Because these two are so closely related, it is important that you spend time with a group of friends even before casually dating so when you begin pairing off you can be as selective as possible.

Learning to Determine Who's Right for You

How can you determine who is the right date for you? That's complicated because each person's needs, background, interests, intellect and ambitions are different. But regardless of personal preference, you'll want to stay away from the situation Larry got himself into.

I know Larry well. When he went to college he wasn't interested in getting serious. He wanted to date young women who didn't have marriage on their minds. That's why he was so pleased when he met Kathy. She was good looking and dating a guy back home, so they could have a good time together and he wouldn't have to worry about her getting serious. Since it was not much fun to go places alone, this arrangement was convenient for both of them.

But the more time they spent together, the more

they enjoyed it. Then summer came and Kathy went back to her old boyfriend, Joe. When school started again, Larry and Kathy took up where they had left off—and their relationship grew without them realizing what was happening. Six months later Kathy broke up with Joe. Kathy and Larry's relationship grew more serious.

Yet something bothered Larry. He had made a list of the characteristics he wanted to have in a future wife, and there were a number of traits Kathy didn't have. He was especially worried about Kathy's emotional instability. Should he keep the relationship growing or should he break up? He took his problem to the Lord.

One night after agonizing over this situation, Larry opened his Bible and his eyes focused on Isaiah 62:5: "And as the bridegroom rejoices over the bride, so shall your God rejoice over you." He took this as an answer to his prayer, an assurance from the Lord that he was to go ahead and marry Kathy.

Their relationship advanced, but every time Kathy went back home and saw Joe, she became confused. She eventually broke up with Larry, but after two weeks she couldn't stand it and begged for him to take her back. He did, thinking that the Bible text was God's assurance that Kathy would someday be his.

Larry and Kathy became engaged. Then summer came and when Kathy once again saw Joe, she was torn. At the end of the summer she broke her engagement to Larry and within months she married Joe. Larry was devastated. Had God failed him?

Later, after Larry fell in love with and married a woman who more closely met his criteria for an ideal wife, he looked back and realized that marrying Kathy would have been a mistake. Her emotional instability would have been like a noose around his neck, zapping all his emotional energy in trying to meet her needs.

There is a triple moral to this true story:

1. Don't steadily date someone just because you're lonely or you don't think you could get serious — unless that person truly is the kind of person you would want to marry someday. It's easy to con yourself into thinking nothing will come of your friendship because the person you are dating is more like a buddy than a girlfriend or boyfriend. But that's not true. And having an old flame back home doesn't necessarily make a person unresponsive to someone nearer. Old flames do die.

2. Don't fall into the trap of putting a fleece before the Lord or claiming a Bible verse to make the decision of a marriage partner for you. God has given you a mind, adequate information, parental counsel and professional help so you can make an intelligent decision. Use them.

3. Don't marry someone who is double-bonded or still in love with another. In other words, don't get married if either one of you has recently broken up with someone else. It takes time to become emotionally detached from a close, long-term, intimate relationship. Kathy never did and Larry suffered because of it. Time is a wonderful healer, but you've got to give it a chance to do its work.

Beware of Being "Needed"

Another moral too many couples learn too late: There are dangers in dating someone who needs you. It's nice to feel needed, but over-dependency doesn't wear well in a marriage relationship. Two happy people usually make a happy marriage. Two needy ones make a marriage that needs much.

John and Phyllis were in my husband's class in college. Phyllis had come from an abusive home. She was defensive and cold. John was a good listener and Phyllis needed a counselor. John spent hours listening to the sordid story of Phyllis's past. He tried to give her the kind of encouragement she needed to get out of the psychological low she was in. His friends, including my husband, couldn't understand why John was investing so much time in Phyllis. They warned him, but he merely laughed at their concern. A year later they were engaged, then married, then had two children, then divorced after seven years.

No one wants to be married to a counselee. It just doesn't work. It's easy for the counselor to get tired of continually being responsible for someone else's happiness or to feel rejected when he is no longer needed. And on the other hand, who wants to be married to a lifetime counselor?

How much better to seek professional counseling *before* marriage so you can enter into a relationship without needless emotional baggage. The best marriage partners are those who have solved personal problems before the wedding ceremony so they can concentrate on giving love to the other rather than selfishly seeing how much they can get.

What You Can (and Cannot) Change

A final moral to consider: You can't change anyone unless they want to change themselves. It's foolish to think that your efforts alone will make the man or woman you are dating into a significantly different person.

Tony was in danger of flunking calculus when he met Tammy, an honor student. Because Tony was a strong, handsome, likeable guy, Tammy was thrilled when he started paying attention to her. She respected his athletic ability, and in spite of his low grades, he seemed intelligent and talked of graduate school. He blamed his grades and low GPA on his lack of interest.

Tammy began tutoring Tony in calculus, which meant they spent many hours together in his apartment. The more time they spent together, the more their feelings for each other grew. Tammy was already madly in love with Tony when it dawned on her that Tony wasn't really as interested in intellectual pursuits as she was. In fact, he probably would never go to graduate school. But she kidded herself into believing that if she could only help him enough, he would change.

Ten years after they were married, Tony was quite comfortable spending his leisure time watching TV and reading the sports section of the paper, while Tammy felt her intellectual self—and her respect for Tony— dying. She admired the sharp intellectual businessmen she worked with, and found it difficult not to compare them to her husband. Plus, she resented Tony for not encouraging her to pursue her own educational goals.

More and more she entertained the thought, *Would my dream of getting a Ph.D. destroy my marriage by creating an even larger intellectual gap between us? If only . . .*

Deep down we all want to be loved unconditionally for who we are. It's unfair to expect major changes from someone who has not given any indication that he or she plans on being any different. Had Tammy looked at her relationship with Tony honestly, she probably would have made a different decision about their marriage.

In summary, don't steadily date someone who is not the type of person you want to marry. And don't marry someone . . .

. . . on blind faith,

. . . who is double-bonded,

. . . who is your counselor or counselee,

. . . who is overly dependent on you to meet his or her needs,

. . . who has unresolved problems of the past,

. . . and don't marry someone whom you think you can change.

All of these morals tell us one thing: Beware of dating yourself into a lopsided love relationship. Remember the biblical counsel not to be unequally yoked together (2 Corinthians 6:14)? Could this instruction be broadly applied beyond the unequal yoking of believers with unbelievers? True love blossoms best in a balanced relationship. It brings a sense of freedom to each partner. With each other's encouragement and support, you can be everything God intended you to be.

❤   ❤   ❤

Something to Think About . . .

It was stated in this chapter that "Being in love is not reason enough to marry." Do you agree or disagree with this statement? What are the dangers in believing "Love conquers all"? What characteristics in a mate will love have a hard time overlooking?

❤ 3 ❤

What Are Your Chances of Beating the Odds?

Research shows that you will have the best chance of staying married — and being happily married — if you marry someone who is similar to you in age, race, cultural values, education, spirituality and interests. It's true that opposites attract, especially where personality is concerned. But when it comes to stability in marriage, it's the similarities, not the differences, that bind individuals together.

Headstrong love makes a couple think they can beat the odds and find happiness and lifelong fulfillment in marriage regardless of what the research says. But before committing your life to another, prayerfully consider your age, racial, cultural, spiritual and educational compatibility. Have you known each other long enough to really know each other? And do you have your parents' support? All these are important factors that will contribute to your marital success.

The Importance of Age

What does age have to do with marital satisfaction? Actually, maturity is far more important to a stable marriage than age, per se. You see, I've met some very immature forty-year-olds!

Young love can work, if you marry the right person. When my brother came back from his twenty-fifth high school reunion, he said that amid all the troubled and broken families, Liz and Gary still behaved like newlyweds. They had married at fifteen and just barely seventeen years of age. Considering the odds, they shouldn't have made it. But they did.

Generally speaking, however, the older you are, the more you have experienced and the wiser you become; therefore, the better your chances will be of choosing a mate most suited for long-term love and commitment. The high school and college years are characterized by rapid change. When couples marry during this time, often their values and interests don't grow together. In addition, younger couples usually don't have the resources to overcome crisis that older couples have (e.g., a good savings account or a support system of mature friends).

Age differences can also affect a marriage. If there is too great a difference in age, not only will there be differences in interests, recreation and friends, but there is also the tendency of one to treat the other like a younger, less responsible person. Some men marry older women because they enjoy being mothered. Women may marry older men because they are unconsciously looking for a father-figure. Mothering and fathering, however, were not meant to be a part of the husband/wife relationship. Parenting may meet a psychological need at first, but it quickly grows old and resentment sets in.

Age differences become less important to older and more mature individuals. It's not unusual for men and women in mid-life to marry a companion that is five to ten years younger or older. In fact, an increasing number of women are marrying younger men. (There may be an advantage to this since men quite often die at an earlier age than women.) Making this choice when you're in high school or college, though, may result in conflict since men generally are not as mature as women during this period.

Remember, it's not the number of birthdays you have had that is important for marital success. It's how mature you are.

Racial Differences

Racial similarity is more important to the ease of marital adjustment than young people tend to believe. Most racially-mixed marriages occur immediately after the couple has been on a high school or college campus where there is a blend of all types of races and cultures and there is a great deal of acceptance of cross-racial dating. But people outside those ivy-covered walls are not usually as generous. It shouldn't be this way, but the fact remains that it is.

After marriage a racially-mixed couple may find that it is more difficult to establish new friendships, especially if they move to a location where their marriage is not as accepted. If the family openly disapproves, this can cause adjustment problems for the couple. Whenever there is a weakening of a couple's support system, there is additional stress placed on the marriage relationship.

When cultural differences are added to racially-mixed marriages, there is even more risk.

Cultural Values

Cultural differences can be like a pesky fly in an otherwise happy union. A person's upbringing determines his or her feelings about values, the way holidays are celebrated, how a woman is treated in the home, how money is handled, the type of language used, what expectations are held for the children, how they should be disciplined, etc.

If you are serious about someone, don't plan a wedding until you have met your future mate's parents. Stay in each other's homes for two or more weeks—you will observe differences you never realized were there. (It's difficult to put on an act for more than a week.) Not until then can you begin asking, "Will I be able to accept these differences? Do we have enough in common that we can adjust to the uncommon?"

My good friend, whom I'll call Jessica, grew up in a warm, accepting, informal southern family who knew no strangers and had a hug for everyone. Dad was gentle, kind and soft-spoken. He had a special love relationship with each child. They could tell him anything and he was never too busy to listen.

Steve had a northern European breeding. Dad was the undisputed head of the family. His word was law. Mom was an excellent cook and homemaker, and was always the one the kids would go to when they needed comforting. Dad rarely took time to read to the children or play with them, and Steve never remembered his dad showing affection to his mom, even though he knew they loved each other. Their lifestyle was just more formal, social events were carefully planned and their physical demonstrations of love were few.

When Jessica spent Thanksgiving vacation at Steve's home, she had a rude awakening. Suddenly she and Steve had a whole new agenda of topics they needed to discuss about the differences between their two families.

It wasn't until Steve visited Jessica's home over Christmas vacation that he really understood what she was talking about. Jessica's family always had a house full of guests, their door was never locked and everyone received a warm, affectionate greeting. Hugging and public demonstrations of affection were hard for Steve. He never remembered his father spontaneously hugging anyone, not even the kids.

Would Steve feel comfortable being the affectionate father Jessica wanted for her children? Would he be the kind of husband who would kiss Jessica or say loving things to her in front of others? And what about spending time with the children? Jessica's idea of parenting was that it should be a shared responsibility. She didn't mind Steve being the head of their home, as long as he discussed everything with her first and they came to a joint decision, as her parents did. She knew she couldn't live happily with someone who considered his word law, regardless of how others felt. Another thing she noticed about Steve's family was that they only talked about business and materialistic things, while her family talked about people, feelings and ideas. Sharing feelings was especially important to Jessica.

Steve, on the other hand, valued more conventional roles. He didn't know whether he could accept the idea of Jessica working outside the home while the children were small.

As it turned out, they got married. Steve liked what he saw in Jessica's home. It was a refreshing change and an eye-opener to him. And if you would talk to Jessica today, she would tell you that Steve is a lot more like her dad than his own. But take note: Not all individuals are able to adjust to another cultural background as easily as Steve did.

The way you are reared, the role models of Mom and Dad, and your cultural heritage will affect your expectations for your marriage. This doesn't imply that these differences make a person less or better than

someone else—just different. How much better to discover these differences before marriage than to resent
them later.

Spirituality

Similarities in spiritual interests and beliefs become extremely important after marriage. A peak is
reached when the kids come along and a decision must
be made about their spiritual instruction. Knowing and
agreeing on where you and your boyfriend or girlfriend
stand spiritually is vital to future marital happiness.

Just belonging to the same denomination is not
enough. There can still be a great disparity in standards and convictions. In fact, there can be greater
differences between two young people from the same
church than there might be between two dedicated
Christians who belong to different denominations.

Your spiritual belief system encompasses every
aspect of your life, including such things as recreation,
entertainment and music. Some denominations have
such a strong heritage of traditions and values con-
cerning things like Sabbath observance, dance, jewelry
or use of tobacco and alcohol that it becomes vitally
important not to marry outside your denomination.

During your courtship, look carefully at your belief
systems. Attend church and study the Bible together.
Discuss the spiritual leadership of the home, and what
role the church will play in your life. Talk about your
concept of God, the nature of Christ, the importance of
righteousness by faith, obedience to the law—including the Ten Commandments. Do you keep one day of
the week holy? Are certain activities considered unacceptable Sabbath activities? What about giving tithe
and offerings? What is your idea about speaking in
tongues, the judgment, the state of the dead, perfec-

tion? Do you believe in a literal coming of Jesus? How does this affect the choices you make now? These are important doctrinal issues that should be discussed before marriage.

Sue married an inactive Jehovah's Witness. Since he didn't attend "church," she never considered the importance of finding out about his belief system before she married him. It was a rude awakening for her when their daughter had surgery and her husband refused to approve the blood transfusion she needed. Even though he wasn't a practicing Witness, this was still a part of his belief system.

Married women report one of the major faults of men is that they don't take religion seriously. Unfortunately, whether a man takes religion seriously is not an issue for many single women. They marry, thinking spiritual similarities don't matter, and then find themselves unequally yoked.

Education

The statistics seem to indicate that the more education you have, the better chance for a successful marriage. It's not, however, the number of years in school or the academic degrees that make marriages happy. It's that the more education a person obtains, the more he learns about himself and the better idea he has about the type of person he wants as a life partner. Plus, hopefully, the more education you get, the older and wiser you become.

Discuss your educational goals. If one partner wants to pursue a graduate degree or professional training, that person will be changing significantly during this period. Many marriages dissolve after one partner puts the other through medical school, law school or a professional course. The more educated partner grows dissatisfied with the lack of self-improvement in the spouse. There is a greater disparity in their interests. This is quite common when wives work so their husbands can advance their professional training. When it's the wife who chooses to go on, a husband may resent the elevated status of her new career or the fact that she now earns more money than he.

Growing together is the key. This doesn't mean if one chooses to get a degree that both should. But both should be willing to continue reading, learning and moving forward on a self-improvement course. Be interested in the work of each other so you can find fulfillment in discussing issues together. In addition, it is important that you help each other move forward toward God's potential for both your lives, rather than using each other merely to further personal goals.

My husband was the one who encouraged me to get my doctorate. He already had his. I had always loved books and learning, but I never thought I could get an advanced degree. I'm sure we could have lived happily with only one doctorate in the family, but having gone through the academic experience myself, we now have much more in common.

Length of Courtship

Research indicates that long courtships (not engagements) are conducive to long marriages. Knowing each other over a long period of time (two years or more) allows you to see each other in many different situations.

Before considering marriage, you will want to observe your loved one in as many different situations as possible. This reduces the surprise factor once you are married.

How does he react when the car breaks down or

someone curses at him or he loses his job? How does she handle the stress of a new job? Does she like to entertain? How are his manners? What's more important to him, Monday night football or a walk in the moonlight with you? How does he treat authority figures?

What really gets her down and how long does it take before she snaps back? Is PMS (premenstrual syndrome) a problem? Does he have frequent headaches? Do you respect his eating habits? Does it bother you that she doesn't take care of her body and exercise?

Is he a show-off in front of his friends? Are you embarrassed by what she says? Will he accept church responsibilities? Does he choose to go hunting and fishing rather than spend extra time with you? Does she use her God-given talents? Does she like to cook? Does he offer to wash the dishes?

How does he keep his room, his clothing, his car and his personal self? How does he feel about government and taxes? What are her political leanings? Does the music he listens to bother you? If she has a free evening, how will she choose to spend it? How does she feel about celebrating Christmas? What does he choose to do on vacation? How does he feel about spending or saving money? Will she buy on credit? And the list could go on and on . . .

The longer you know each other, the more chances you will have to observe each other in a wide variety of situations. A longer courtship gives you time to discuss your differences and be willing either to compromise or establish more cohesive habit patterns. It isn't impossible to change after marriage—it's just more difficult than before.

Parental Acceptance

Parental approval is another contribution to a lasting marriage. Few people know a child as well as the parents do. Of course, parents make mistakes. They can have unrealistic expectations and object to their child's choice of a mate because they really don't know the person. Or they may have a hang-up about the person not having musical or athletic ability. But on the whole, if parents are against the relationship, this should be a caution light to you.

Look carefully at your developing relationship. Seek the counsel of other trusted adults. Talk earnestly with your parents about their concerns. Listen respectfully without becoming defensive. Fast and pray to determine the truth of their observations. And don't rush the relationship. Time has a way of working things out. Either your parents' insights will become apparent to you, or they will realize that their concerns were groundless.

There is one exception to this rule—the Christian couple who is having to deal with the irrational opinions of non-Christian parents. If time doesn't heal this schism, the couple should seek the advice of a pastor or other spiritual leaders. If you decide to go ahead and get married, try not to antagonize your parents. Make your intentions clear and be willing to live with the consequences.

True love should not cause a conflict with the family. It's the physical, infatuation-type love that can cause major dissension, especially when parents are trying to counsel their children and the young couple feel they know better, hurtfully rejecting their parents and their advice. These wounds may take years to heal.

At one of my seminars, Shelly's mom told me this story. Shelly and her parents were extremely close during her growing-up years, and the folks carefully monitored the boyfriends who showed up on their doorstep.

But college away from home brought added freedom and Shelly began to date some questionable characters—at least her parents thought so. At first Shelly freely confided in her parents: "Hey, I've just met this really great guy named Michael. He's smart—a Merit Scholar—and comes from a wealthy family in Florida. Ah, he has, kind of like, purple hair. He's really a nice guy, though, and so athletic. When you see him, I hope you don't mind the ring in his ear."

Well, you can imagine the parents' reaction. So Shelly went underground with her dating. She ended up with a guy who didn't have purple hair and an earring, but he did have a rebellious and dominating spirit. He became possessive of Shelly. He resented her even calling her parents because every time she did, their concern and counsel left her confused. Word leaked through to Mom and Dad that this guy was on drugs and not enrolled in classes, even though he masqueraded as a student.

After a home visit, Shelly went back to college determined to break up, but her boyfriend wouldn't listen. Instead, he talked Shelly into living in his mother's house where she could be "protected" from her parents' interference. His mom wouldn't even let Shelly's folks talk to her on the phone.

Six months later Shelly woke up to the fact that she was being manipulated by this possessive guy. She moved out, and thanked her parents for their continuing prayers. Shelly's parents were more than a little relieved she didn't marry this man.

The old cliché is true: When you marry, you marry the family. Why start out marriage with bitter feelings against parents and in-laws? With a little more time, relational differences are likely to resolve themselves. According to the Scriptures, true love never fails (1 Corinthians 13:8). If your love is true, it will pass the test of time until parents accept your union.

Studies verify the importance of age, race, parental approval, cultural values, education and spiritual interests when it comes to having a marriage that lasts. "But," say young lovers, "we're not statistics. We're not like everyone else. We'll never get a divorce." There are exceptions to every rule, that's true. However, your chances for a happy, lifelong marriage are greater if these factors are considered carefully.

Trying to beat the odds is risky business in a world where Satan would like nothing better than to break up a home, destroying husband, wife and children in the process. Proverbs 3:4-6 is good counsel to those who are serious about love:

> If you want favor with both God and man, and a reputation for good judgment and common sense, then trust the Lord completely; don't ever trust yourself. In everything you do, put God first, and he will direct you and crown your efforts with success (TLB).

❤   ❤   ❤

Something to Think About . . .

Have you and the person you're dating discussed your differences in the areas mentioned in this chapter? Do you see any points of potential conflict? In what ways are you alike? Plan now to set aside time this month to talk about these issues.

♥ 4 ♥

Qualities of a Great Date

You've probably thought a lot about your future mate. You may have described him or her in vague generalities, or perhaps you've gotten specific about the type of person you'd like to marry. I believe everybody should make a list of essential characteristics they want in a mate. Before reading this chapter, why don't you take a minute to make your own list? Compare your list to the traits I'll be talking about, adding any characteristics you feel you may have missed.

The Traits I Want in a Mate

1.	11.
2.	12.
3.	13.
4.	14.
5.	15.
6.	16.
7.	17.
8.	18.
9.	19.
10.	20.

Take a good look at your list and then remind yourself you'll never find a "perfect" mate because there is no such thing! We're human beings, after all. You need to decide which of the things you have listed are absolutely essential and which could be considered frosting on the cake. You can do this by either ranking your list, putting the most important traits at the top, or by breaking your list into two categories: those traits that are absolutely essential, and those that would be nice but not absolutely necessary.

**Traits Ranked
in Order of Importance** or **Essential Traits**

1.	1.
2.	2.
3.	3.
4.	4.
5.	5.
6.	6.
7.	7.
8.	8.
9.	9.
10.	10.

Finished? Let's move ahead.

The following are some traits I think are important for a good marriage partner to have. How do you feel?

Trait 1: A Happy Disposition

Look for a happy, optimistic person. Find someone who has a sense of humor and can laugh at himself. It's not much fun to live with a negative, critical, pessimistic, complaining person or someone who habitually puts you, himself or others down. True happiness springs from a content heart. Beware of the person who is only happy when you are around. You're going to get tired of being responsible for another person's happiness. You could end up feeling guilty when that person slips into bouts of depression. It's easy to blame yourself and say, "If I were only a better person, she would be happy."

And beware of the date who says, "I will be happy if you marry me, shave off your beard, lose five pounds and get a new car." True happiness is not dependent on "things." It's a part of a person's character, regardless of the circumstances.

If you think you're going to change a pessimist into an optimist, forget it. Lifetime habits of negative thinking won't change overnight. These negative traits can be repressed during the romance of a courtship, so the only way you will know if a real change has occurred is not to rush to the altar. Marry a happy person. Don't marry one that merely promises happiness.

Trait 2: Thoughtfulness

This is the trait that first made me sit up and take note of Jan—the man I would someday marry. Jan's sister, Chris, had an old clunker of a car. I'll never forget the night we took Jan back to the airport after our "blind" first date. He was in his business suit, white starched shirt and tie. As he got out of the car he said to his sister, "Chris, let me check your oil." I couldn't believe it! I had never heard of a guy being that thoughtful of his sister. Suddenly, I was interested.

How does your date treat his parents and yours? Chances are you'll get treated very much the same way. Does she see things that need to be done and offer to help? Or does he put his own needs first? Does he open the car door and wait to seat you at the table? Manners are important—and they seldom get better after marriage.

Trait 3: Not Easily Angered

George was a talented, handsome guy, but he couldn't seem to control his anger. Little things set him off. For a while Missy put up with his "mini" temper tantrums, like blasting the horn when a car cut in too close, or yelling at his mother, "Don't tell me what to do!"

Missy tried to make excuses for his behavior, thinking he was tired since he had a full-time job and was going to business school on the side. When she finally brought up the subject of his temper, he got angry.

One night when George took Missy out to dinner, he discovered he didn't have any cash in his wallet. He had I.D., but the restaurant wouldn't accept a check and policy was policy. George argued, pounded his fist on the table and finally yelled, "Get me the manager!" Missy was embarrassed, left the restaurant and broke the engagement.

Missy's decision was a wise one. Temper outbursts like this can be the symptom of internal hostility. This hostility is often repressed during courtship as a person is trying hard to be on his best behavior, but it will become more frequent and more violent after marriage. Take seriously any outburst you observe, and check with others who have known this person in different situations to see if they have noticed this trait.

Do not marry a man with a history of hitting his mother, sister or another woman in a temper outburst. If it happened once, it can happen again, and after marriage you or your children are likely to be the victims. Anger can also cause a wife to be abusive to her husband or family. The way a woman treats her younger brother may be an indication of how she will treat her husband.

Anger can be expressed in many ways, and the angry outbursts or temper tantrums that George expressed are simply the most easily recognizable. Be equally leery of the person who has not learned to express anger in words and instead merely harbors angry feelings in his heart. Going silent and withdrawing from a loved one because of anger is unhealthy and damaging to a relationship. It's rejection par excellence.

Everyone experiences feelings of anger. The secret is to recognize the first signs and be willing to deal with the anger in a constructive way by talking it out, playing a good game of tennis or cleaning the oven. Don't allow angry feelings to build, causing an uncontrolled explosion or a hostile silence.

Discovering the root of internal hostility and learning to solve problems without anger usually takes professional counseling. The motivation for a guy like George to seek the help he needs to overcome his destructive behavior will be much greater before marriage than after.

Be sure you date a person long enough to observe how easily he or she becomes angry and how these angry feelings are expressed. Ask yourself, "Is this what I want to live with for a lifetime?"

Trait 4: Willing to Solve Problems

If you went by looks, Kent was probably the most desirable guy on campus: robust with gorgeous blue eyes and wavy dark hair. But his behavior was not nearly as attractive as his appearance. You see, Kent was never wrong—at least according to his own opinion. If mistakes were made, it was always the other guy's fault. He never said, "I'm sorry," because he wasn't. He was always right. Why solve problems? That would mean admitting that something was wrong. And compromise was out of the question.

When Kent started dating Julie, he thought he had found the perfect woman. She was gentle and hated conflict, so when they had a difference of opinion, she backed down. Sometimes she tried to reason with him and suggested a compromise, but her words fell on deaf ears. It didn't take her long to discover that they got along much better when she just accepted what he said and didn't argue.

They would have never gotten married had Julie realized that Kent wasn't going to change, or had Kent realized that Julie was. As Julie's self-confidence increased, she began to stand up to Kent. She learned that she could get her own way and avoid a conflict by merely doing things behind Kent's back.

And the result? A miserable marriage. When things hit a low, Julie threatened to leave unless they got counseling. "Counseling?" exclaimed Kent. "Who needs counseling? There's nothing wrong with me!"

It's almost impossible to solve relationship problems by yourself. Marry someone who will be honest enough to admit being wrong, who doesn't have a habit of blaming others, and who is interested in solving problems. Marry someone who believes that God's way means submission to one another (Ephesians 5:21) and not just the wife to her husband.

Trait 5: Purity

Purity is not just an old-fashioned virtue. It's becoming more and more in vogue since the threat of AIDS. It's just safer to date someone who hasn't played around. Plan now the circumstances under which you want to first have sex. If it's on your wedding night with your marriage partner, giving each other your gift of virginity, you should seriously consider the wisdom of dating someone who has already chosen to give his or her gift away.

At the same time you should not hold it against a person for past sexual involvement. Rebellion, ignorance or being taken advantage of can rob a person of his or her virginity. Statistics tell us that even among Christian young adults, many have been involved in premarital sex. The important questions to ask are: What is my date's current commitment to purity? What were the circumstances of that previous sexual encounter? Was the sexual experience a revelation of true character that is being masked at this moment, or was it a mistake that the person feels deeply sorry for and has vowed not to repeat? Choosing from this moment on to keep yourself for your marriage partner will make your wedding night special.

You cannot always judge a person's true purity by virginity alone. It has been estimated that at least one-fourth of all women have suffered sexual abuse or incest in childhood, and perhaps as many as one-sixth of all men. We accept the fact that rape is all too common among young women, but we don't often consider that young boys and men are also sexually violated against their wishes.

If this has happened to you, you are not at fault. You did not choose this. You may have been the victim of a sexual experience, but this does not have to destroy your purity. However, this abuse can affect your future relationships unless you seek professional help.

If you are dating someone who has been sexually violated, don't get married unless that person has received counseling and expresses a willingness to get further counseling if remnants of the past begin to affect the marriage relationship. If you are engaged, the counselor may want to talk to both of you so you can gain insight into how this might affect your future. Problems relating to sexual abuse often don't surface until the sexual experience in marriage triggers past memories. Commit now to seeking counseling in the future should the need arise.

Mind purity is equally important. Is your date pure in his or her thoughts and speech, as well as behavior? What jokes does he tell? What music does she listen to? What movies does he watch? What books or magazines does she read? Are they pure or suggestive? Mind pollution can lead to disrespect of the opposite sex. You don't want to marry a crude, immoral individual.

Trait 6: Truthful

Too often couples play games when they are becoming acquainted. "I can't act as if I like him, because that would be too forward." "If I told him the truth, he might not like me." "I hate rock music, but I pretend it's okay because I don't want to hurt her feelings." Playing games in a relationship is a form of dishonesty. As long as games are being played, don't get serious.

Marriage isn't a game. It's a serious lifetime commitment. Your marriage will never pass the test of time if it is built on the sands of dishonesty. Search your own feelings and share honestly during your courtship. *Be you.* If what you say or what you do is misunderstood, how much better it is to find that out before you get married and have to suffer through a lifetime of misunderstanding.

Some people are habitual liars—a very serious character flaw. They lie without thinking and for no apparent reason. It will be impossible to build a stable marriage with a person who is basically untrustworthy.

But just how truthful should you and your date be about past behavior? What if you have had a drug or alcohol addiction or have served time? Should you mention you had been sexually active? Maybe you have been the victim of rape or abuse. Should the person you date be burdened with these facts? Each individual will have to determine when the specifics of his or her past behavior need to be revealed.

Casual dating does not require full disclosure. Only you can determine how much to tell. Usually details are not necessary. It may be enough to say honestly, "I'm not proud of everything I did in my past, but I would like to put that behind me and be judged for the person I have become. If our relationship continues to grow and we are considering a lifetime commitment to each other, then I think it would be important that we share anything in our pasts that might affect our future relationship."

Honesty, tempered with common sense, is the best policy. If you have a question about how much to tell, seek the advice of a counselor rather than your friends.

Trait 7: Good Health Habits

No one wants to marry a slob—and few do. The end result of poor health habits usually doesn't show up during the early twenties or thirties. By forty and fifty, though, such things as overeating, snacking between meals, little or no exercise, and smoking begin to take their toll. Too often people end up married to health problems that could have been prevented.

Seven health habits have been isolated as important for longevity. Look for someone who (1) sleeps approximately seven to eight hours out of twenty-four (too little or too much sleep may be a symptom of other problems), (2) eats breakfast, (3) doesn't eat between meals, (4) keeps a moderate weight—not too fat or too thin, (5) exercises, (6) doesn't smoke and (7) doesn't drink.

As you hold hands with the campus beauty queen or stare into the eyes of the football hero, it is difficult to imagine being married to an unattractive, over-weight, unconditioned person. But it can happen to you, unless you marry someone who practices good health habits.

Health habits are a very personal matter. What one may consider good health habits may not be good enough for another. For one, a twenty minute walk a day is adequate. For another, nothing less than five miles of jogging will do. For one, it is enough to eat lean meat and only a sip of alcohol at social occasions. For another, good health means a non-junk food, vegetarian diet with no preservatives, sugar or alcohol.

Because alcoholism can devastate a marriage, consider carefully a person's view of drinking. Most people don't know they have married an alcoholic until some type of stress triggers an increase in alcohol consumption. The safest policy is to look for someone who doesn't drink and is not tempted to do so.

If you are engaged to someone who has grown up in an alcoholic home, it would be wise to attend together a series of Alanon classes (Alcoholics Anonymous for family members). Go to a counselor trained in substance abuse to discuss how this back-ground concerns your future marriage. Alcoholism has significant and long-lasting effects on family members.

Drug abuse is equally harmful. Beware of the person who feels pills are the acceptable way to feel good, keep awake, go to sleep or whatever else. Taking medication for every occasion can easily become a habit and lead to more addictive drugs which alter moods and behavior. It's best not to mess around with drugs, even those which can be purchased over the counter.

Bad health habits are difficult to break. That is why it's best to look for a person who has already established positive health practices. Health habits, including the simple acts of brushing and flossing teeth, or the frequency of bathing, are important contributors to marital happiness.

Trait 8: Accepts Responsibility

For six of the eight years Tiffany and Jim have been married, Jim hasn't had a job. At first Tiffany tried to blame Jim's erratic work history on his not finding the right job. But now, with two preschoolers and Jim once again jobless, Tiffany knows that's not the case. At least she expected Jim to take care of the home responsibilities while he was unemployed, but he didn't.

Jim is just a happy-go-lucky kind of a person who doesn't like to be tied down to anything, especially not an eight-to-five job or the responsibilities of children. Eight years into her marriage, Tiffany is sure she wouldn't have married Jim if she had realized just how irresponsible he was. But how could she have known?

Here are some questions that might detect irresponsibility:

Does he finish classes and projects he starts? Does she choose to complete homework and study for exams rather than party? Has he ever held a steady job? Does she see things that need to be done and do them? Does he volunteer to help? Does she get to places on time? Does he make lame excuses to get out of responsibilities? Does she take her talents seriously and work to improve her skills? Does he take care of his car and

other personal possessions? Does she brag about getting out of work?

Think about it. Just how responsible is the person
you are dating?

Trait 9: Good Sense of Self-Worth

Clint talks about himself and how great he is. Lori
always puts herself down. Todd is a name dropper.
Jessie won't try anything new. Marta withdraws when
she is in group situations. Tim is constantly asking for
affirmation, "How do you think I did?" Frank is a gossip.
Leslie has a knack for slamming others and pouting.
James is always getting his feelings hurt.

What do all these people have in common? They
are all suffering from a poor self-concept. People with
a low sense of self-worth don't make good marriage
partners.

Often in a dating relationship, individuals with a
poor self-esteem glean a sense of value from the person
they're with. They become dependent on their date to
make them feel good. Sometimes they become like
leeches, wanting the full attention of their date and
resenting it when he or she interacts with others.

Individuals with a negative self-concept sometimes have difficulty supporting and encouraging
others. In some twisted way they think that if another
person becomes successful, it will make them look
worse. Some men suffer when their wives get a career
promotion or make more money, for example. Some
women cringe when their husbands are the life of the
party. They resent the fact that the man they married
has a great personality that just naturally attracts
attention.

Tory was attracted to Heather because of her skill
at the keyboard. They were both music majors and they

had a lot in common. Tory felt Heather was good for him because he had to practice hard to keep up with her. As their relationship developed, however, Tory grew resentful of Heather's natural talent and began competing with her for recognition and praise. Heather wondered why he never praised or encouraged her. She was really hurt when word got back to her that Tory had been critical of her recital performance. At that point, red flags began to fly. Heather decided to discontinue the relationship, even though everybody thought they were perfect for each other because of their similar interests.

The next quarter Heather began dating a biology major. Rob knew very little about music, but he could sit for hours and listen to Heather play. He encouraged her, and even made some contacts for her which resulted in a recording contract with an established studio. It wasn't long before Heather realized she was falling for this guy. This frightened her, since she had always pictured herself marrying someone musical.

When she talked to the dean of women about her dilemma, the wise woman said, "The secret to a successful marriage is to find someone who compliments you, not competes with you. You should only marry when each of you feels so comfortable with your own talents that you can help the other become the very best he or she can be. You want a marriage partner who will help you reach your potential, not sabotage your efforts." That's good advice.

If you don't want to live a lifetime having to tiptoe around a person's fragile ego or having to hold yourself back for fear of how your spouse will react, then be careful not to get emotionally involved with someone who has a low sense of self-worth.

A person's self-concept can change. We all, at times, have suffered from feelings of inadequacy.

Professional counseling is recommended if one is plagued with persistent feelings of inferiority or inflated superiority—both are caused by a low self-concept. A positive sense of worth is vital for marital happiness. Don't marry without it.

Trait 10: Likes Children

You may think you'll never have children—but don't bet on it. If you do, you'll discover that a marriage will either be weakened or strengthened by kids. Finding someone who likes children, understands them, and enjoys having them around is a real plus, if you want to have both a happy marriage—and children.

Ted was a perfectionist. One time when he and Lisa were dating, a couple of little children came over to his car and touched it with their sticky fingers. Ted had a fit! He plowed those kids down with a stream of harsh adjectives as they fled from the scene. Later when they were visiting Lisa's older sister and her baby started to cry, Ted complained, "Why can't they keep that kid quiet?"

When Lisa asked him how he felt about children, he shrugged his shoulders and said, "They're okay when they stay in their place." That was enough for Lisa. She loved children and wanted to find a mate who felt the same way. Ted just didn't measure up.

Studies show that couples with children are often less satisfied with their marriages than couples without children. The reason for this is twofold. First, it takes time to meet the needs of children. Parents sometimes neglect their needs as a couple because they are so busy with their children. Second, it's easy to disagree over how children should be raised. Before marriage you may discuss children, but unless you're around a lot of children and can observe your date interacting with them in a wide variety of situations, you really don't have any idea about how he or she may discipline your children in the future. Seldom do both parents totally agree on how a child should be raised. Finding someone who at least likes children is an advantage.

Trait 11: A Personal Relationship With God

It's very important for a marriage partner to have a personal relationship with God. Look for someone who is spiritually sensitive and willing to follow God's law. A Spirit-filled life is one filled with love, joy, peace, patience, gentleness, goodness, faith, meekness and temperance (Galatians 5:22,23). A person who exhibits these traits is certainly easier to live with than someone who doesn't.

Beware of the person who gets spiritual just to win your affection or someone who says he loves the Lord, but doesn't act like it. You want to marry someone with a genuine Christian experience. Does your date talk about God? Can you discuss religious issues? Does he or she ever mention personal devotions? Do you ever see your date holding or reading a Bible? Do you enjoy going to religious meetings together? Does he have any speech or behavior patterns that seem inconsistent with a dedicated Christian? Can you pray together? Does being together help you grow spiritually?

Traci wasn't much interested in God when she first met Todd, and that's why she was nearly blown off her feet on their first date. After getting in his car to drive to a restaurant, Todd said, "I'd just like to ask the Lord to bless the time we spend together."

It didn't take Traci long to realize that Todd's faith was an integral part of him, not just something he put on for the weekend. And she liked it.

What about your date? If you're interested in a real Christian, make sure his faith is part of his life twenty-four hours a day.

Trait 12: Accepts You Just the Way You Are

No one wants to go through life like a puppet on a string, constantly trying to win the approval of a marriage partner. Nor do you want to be the puppeteer pulling all the strings. If you go into marriage thinking you can change your mate, you'll be like the puppeteer and your poor partner will be your puppet.

True love is unconditional love. This means that you are loved and accepted just the way you are, regardless of how fat you are, what you eat, how you keep the house, whether you have a high-paying job, or whether you slaughter your mother tongue. Not until you love a person unconditionally, and you feel loved the same way, should you ever consider marriage.

Never marry a person just because you love his or her strengths. Loving good traits comes naturally. The important question to ask is, "Do I love her faults?" Only when you can truly love the total person, including all the weak points and bad habits, can you accept your mate for who he is and not secretly wish you could change him.

Shy away from the person who thinks he or she can improve you, and without asking your permission puts you on an improvement plan. Watch the gal who is always straightening your tie or picking lint off your jacket. Be careful of that guy who tells you the right way to do something, or is always correcting your speech. If this picky behavior is irritating before marriage, you can bet it will only get significantly worse afterward.

Trait 13: Willing to Grow

You will want to marry someone who is willing and capable of growing at a similar rate as you. Hopefully this person is interested in reading self-improvement books, asking advice of experienced individuals, counseling with professionals if there is a need, attending marriage, birthing or child-rearing classes, or joining growth groups.

Marriage is never static. Good marriage partners grow together. They encourage each other to maximize their knowledge, skills and potential. You can never know enough on your wedding day to get you smoothly through the various stages and crises of the family life cycle. Make sure the person you date seriously is the kind of person who is open to learning and will make changes when changes need to be made.

Trait 14: Affectionate

I mention this characteristic last, not because it is the least important (it may be the most important), but because this trait may be difficult to assess on a casual dating basis, and may be misunderstood during more serious dating.

The ability to express love through words and actions is vital for an intimate love relationship. Sex without affection is merely an act. It may satisfy an immediate desire, but it doesn't build intimacy. Ann Landers conducted a survey on the importance of close, tender affection versus sex in the lives of women. When asked if they would be content to be held close and treated tenderly and forget about "the act," the majority of women (72 percent) said yes. Even women under forty voted for affection above sex.

Lucy's experience (I've changed her name to protect her identity) is just one example. She once told me, "I was brought up in a strict home where my folks frowned on too much affection in a dating relationship. So when I became engaged, I just thought it was natural that my fiance and I didn't express very much affection for each other. Once we were married, though, I expected things to be different. I needed expressions of affection, and was shocked and bitterly disappointed when my husband didn't change after marriage.

"He just was not an affectionate person. He never received affection as a child, so he didn't know how to give it. And he wouldn't allow me to be affectionate with him. Needless to say, I spent many lonely nights crying myself to sleep. Things got worse when the children came along. I don't ever remember him telling them that they were loved. And hugging and kissing were just not a part of his nature."

What happened to Lucy's marriage? Twenty years later it fell apart. Affection is like glue in a marriage. Without it, it's almost impossible to hold a relationship together. When Lucy considered remarriage, she looked specifically for a warm, affectionate man.

How can you assess whether the person you are dating is an affectionate person when his or her lack of affection may merely be a wise choice to keep the relationship from advancing faster than your rationality? Or how can you make sure the affection that is shown to you is not just physical attraction being used as a powerful tool to entice you for sexual favors?

The answer is to look for tender words, acts and touches that are given naturally *and appropriately* throughout the day, and not just in private to initiate petting.

Appropriate affection is extremely important. One of my friends told me that his son brought a girlfriend home for Christmas who spent the whole vacation crawling all over him. It was sickening and highly inappropriate. The father worried how much longer his young son was going to be able to withstand such an onslaught of affection. If this was the way they acted in public, what must it be like in private?

This shallow affection is hot and passionate on a short-term basis only, and rarely continues after marriage—or after the person gets what he or she wants.

Another way to assess how the person you're dating feels about affection is to discuss how affection was shown in each of your families. How did your folks feel about touch? Was there much hugging and kissing among family members? Talk about your individual needs for affection and the type of affection you both want in a marriage relationship. As you advance toward marriage, you'll also want to talk frankly about the relationship between affection and sex.

Each person will value the traits mentioned in this chapter differently, and there are many more that could be added to your list. Discuss with the person you're seriously dating what you consider essential characteristics in a marriage partner. It will give you some important insights into each other.

One last thing. You may be wondering where looks rank in a list of essential traits. I admit, looks are important, especially a neat and well-groomed appearance. Personally, I'd shy away from the guy with purple hair and an earring, and I'm not so sure most men would be attracted to a woman who is eighty pounds overweight. *But looks can change!*

What's really important is what's on the inside. Far too many young people use appearance as a sole criterion for judging a potential date. In doing so, they overlook individuals who would make great marriage partners. Why don't you do the uncommon thing and leave looks off your list? Concentrate on other essential traits. Chances are you'll be surprised how attractive a person becomes when you see the beauty of his or her character.

❤ ❤ ❤

Something to Think About . . .

Is your list of traits finished? How do the people you date fare when compared to your list? What traits are optional? What traits are non-negotiable? In prayer, offer your list to the Lord, asking Him to work in the life of the person you will eventually marry.

♥ 5 ♥

How to Be a Great Mate

Finding the right person will not necessarily insure marital happiness; being the right mate, however, may. So before going in search of your "Mr. Right" or "Ms. Everything," why don't you take a good look at yourself and ask, "Would I make a great mate?" First of all, how do you measure up on the fourteen traits mentioned in the last chapter?

1. Do you have a happy disposition?

2. Are you thoughtful?

3. Are you not easily angered?

4. Are you willing to solve problems?

5. Are your thoughts and behavior pure?

6. Are you truthful?

7. Do you practice good health habits?

8. Are you responsible?

9. Do you have a good sense of self-worth?

10. Do you like children?

11. Do you have a personal relationship with God?

12. Do you unconditionally accept others just the way they are without trying to change them?

13. Are you willing to grow?

14. Do you show appropriate affection?

What does it take to be a great mate? All of the above, plus! That's a pretty tall order, isn't it? In fact, it's probably easier to *find* the right mate than to *be* the right mate. Being the right mate means the chances are good you're going to have to make some changes in your life.

Let's take a look at some of the qualities you'll need in order to be the right mate for someone special. Keep in mind that no one can be perfect in all these areas— just be willing to grow and change toward the ideal.

Valuing and Accepting Yourself

People who make great marriage partners don't have to be married to be happy. They are happy just being themselves. They are complete in Jesus Christ and feel comfortable with themselves. They like themselves.

Wait a minute. Doesn't that sound too self-sufficient? Shouldn't marriage partners need each other? Well, yes—and no.

Yes, they should need each other but only because they enjoy meeting each other's needs. And no, they shouldn't be dependent on each other for their needs to be met.

Partners in a dependent relationship are skating through marriage on thin ice. What if something happens and one marriage partner can no longer meet the needs of the other? Is there enough unselfish love available that the marriage won't come unglued?

Look at it this way. Let's say you marry someone because that person makes you feel comfortable when you are in public and you need that feeling of security. But what happens when that person has to go away on a trip and you must attend a social function alone? Will you resent your spouse leaving you at that time? Will you complain and make life miserable every time business takes him or her out of town?

If you need someone's presence in order to feel secure and comfortable, you are likely to try to keep that person as close to you as possible. While being able to meet your need makes your spouse feel good at first, six months down the marital highway this dependency is likely to become a burden. Your mate may post an emancipation proclamation and start fighting for freedom.

How can you be sure that you don't marry another person because you need that person? Concentrate on valuing and accepting yourself. You can only accept and value someone else as much as you accept and value yourself. If you don't like who you are, the chances are great that you will try to find a partner who makes you feel better about yourself. You use that person to meet your unmet needs, and that's how unhealthy emotional dependency begins.

To avoid emotional dependency, concentrate on developing self-value and acceptance. Here's how to get started.

Understand How Valuable You Are to God

God considers you a person of immeasurable worth. Take some time to read and study what the Bible has to say about you. You'll discover that you are valuable because:

• God created you (Psalm 139:13-16).

- God knew you and what you would become before your birth (Jeremiah 1:5).

- Jesus died to save you. In fact, He would have died just for you (John 3:16).

- God is preparing a home in heaven for you (John 14:1-3).

- God calls you His child (1 John 3:1).

- God needs you to represent His character to the universe (Job 1:6-8).

- Christ changes our lives by covering our "filthy-rag righteousness" with His robe of righteousness (Isaiah 64:6).

Look up the following verses and see how they make you feel. To make the experience even more meaningful, read these passages from a number of different versions. If there is a verse you find encouraging, why don't you memorize it?

Psalm 8:3-5	Galatians 2:20
Jeremiah 29:11	Philippians 3:20,21
Jeremiah 31:3	Philippians 4:13
Zephaniah 3:17	1 John 3:2
Matthew 17:20	1 John 3:24
Luke 15:8-10	1 John 5:19

Realize That Nobody's Perfect

If you doubt God's acceptance of you because you aren't perfect and don't feel worthy, check out the following texts:

- Psalm 18:30—"As for God, His way is perfect." (It doesn't say we have to be.)

- Matthew 19:21—Jesus told the rich young ruler if he wanted to be perfect, he was to give everything to the poor and follow Him. Jesus knew that this man had put his worldly possessions in front of his love for God. According to Christ, the way to "perfection" is to put God first, and follow Him. It doesn't mean never making another mistake.

- John 17:23—Without Jesus within us we can't be perfect.

- Colossians 1:28—Paul says the reason they preach Christ is so everyone can be presented perfect in Christ. (Outside of Christ, perfection doesn't exist.)

- Hebrews 7:19—The law (or doing right things) makes no one perfect.

- Hebrews 12:23—Men are made perfect. (They don't get that way themselves.)

- James 3:2—We all make mistakes. If we didn't, James says, we'd be perfect. (His assumption seems to be that no one is perfect.)

The above texts may seem to contradict what Jesus said in Matthew 5:48, "Therefore you shall be perfect, just as your Father in heaven is perfect." However, read this passage in context. Jesus is delivering His Sermon on the Mount and has just given guidelines on how people should behave toward their enemies. He says if we can love our enemies (which is probably the hardest thing in the world to do), we'll be perfect because that's the way God is. It doesn't say that perfection is the ticket to God's acceptance.

Just look at David, who was called a man after God's own heart (1 Samuel 13:14), and you'll realize perfection isn't a requirement in God's kingdom. David seduced a woman, got her pregnant, had her husband killed and then lied about it. Obviously it wasn't his behavior that made him a man after God's own heart. Rather, it was his attitude of repentance without casting blame and his ultimate desire to have God create a new heart within him (Psalm 51:10) that drew him close to God.

Take an Honest Look at Yourself

Write down all the traits you like and dislike about yourself.

Traits I like about myself	Traits I dislike about myself

Now compare your two lists. Which one is longer? You might show your list of traits you dislike about yourself to one or two trusted friends for their confirmation. If they don't see some of your traits negatively, you may have been too hard on yourself.

Now take your "dislike" list and think of one thing you could do to help you overcome each negative trait. If you are actively working on a self-improvement plan, you will feel better about yourself. *Warning:* Don't try to be perfect. It's the process of working toward becoming a better person that counts, not the ability to never make a mistake.

Post your "like" list in a place where you will see it often, such as your bathroom mirror. Each time you see it, read it and say, "Thanks, Lord, for making me with these traits." God made you special. How must He feel when you don't value His creation?

Evaluate Your Progress

Periodically, evaluate how well you are doing on developing self-value (through Christ) and self-acceptance. You can do this by asking two questions. The first: *Do I value others?* You can't value and accept others unless you value and accept yourself. Don't think about marriage until you can unselfishly serve others, putting their needs above your own. Marriage requires this type of self-sacrifice.

The second question is: *Am I willing to grow?* When you value and accept yourself, you will have the courage to begin making changes in your life. It's always easier to see how others should change than to muster the energy it takes to change yourself. But marriage requires change from you. You can no longer live a selfish existence. Because you knit your life together with another person, everything you do will affect your marriage partner, and everything he or she does will affect you. To blend your lives together into one is going to mean that you both must be willing to compromise. And you both must be willing to change.

Can you accept the fact that you aren't perfect? A

willingness to change for the better makes you great mate material.

Dealing With the Pathology of Your Past

Bob is a forty-six-year-old physician who has been married and divorced twice. He once commented to me that both of his marital failures could have been prevented if he had received the psychological help he needed before his first marriage. "Love is not enough to overcome personal pathology," he said.

After the break-up of his second marriage, he was devastated. In the depth of his despair he sought help. During the process of counseling he was given a battery of personality tests, and when he looked at the results he was stunned. He went off the scale on the dominance factor. He knew he had an internal need to control, but he just thought it was normal.

In talking about his childhood to a counselor, he discovered the roots of this pathology. His parents were eastern Europeans who came to this country when he was six. Whatever his mother said, he did. If not, he knew his father would belt him. He hated this and grew to resent his parents controlling his life. In fact, he resented anyone controlling his life. He developed an attitude that whatever his parents wanted him to do, he'd do the opposite. He said his younger brother was the same way. The folks wanted his brother to become a physician, but instead he took nuclear physics. His brother has never really been happy in his career choice, but he would never admit it to his parents.

When Bob first came to this country, he was teased by the other kids in school because he didn't know the language and behaved in a culturally different manner. He soon found, though, he could control his peers by cool, calculated, stand-off behavior that caused others to become uncomfortable and finally give in to him. Because of this, many of his acquaintances thought he was stuck-up. He tried not to let their criticism hurt by convincing himself they were wrong and he was right. He thus became highly opinionated and would not give up until he convinced others he was right. He also developed a need to always have the best. If he could flaunt high-fashion clothing, the best car, an expensive watch or tennis racket, other people would notice and accept him.

The problem came when he carried this pathology into marriage. He chose a woman who was a very popular and talented campus leader. Throughout the courtship he was always fearful of losing her to someone more in her league, so he never left her side and spoke quite negatively about her friends. After marriage his need to control became even stronger. If she didn't do what he wanted, he tried to control her with his anger or he withdrew his love. As her respect for him diminished, she grew stronger in her defiance and began exerting her own will. This brought tension and conflict. And the result? During one of his "pouting" times, she found someone who accepted her and she had an affair.

The sad fact is that Bob's second marriage was almost an exact repeat of the first. How unfortunate it was that Bob and his first wife didn't have more intensive premarital counseling. Such counseling would have brought his pathology (and perhaps some of hers) to the surface so it could be dealt with and healed before it destroyed the marriage. But then, Bob and his fiance were so "in love" and emotionally dependent on each other, they probably wouldn't have listened.

When Perfect Isn't Good Enough

Another area of pathology many people suffer from is perfectionism. A perfectionist is a person who isn't satisfied with excellence—he wants more. He attempts the impossible and then feels guilty when he can't attain it.

Tiffany struggled with these feelings all her life. She was a physically beautiful child, highly intellectual and multi-talented. Everyone expected miracles out of her because she could produce them. She began to feel she had to be perfect to be accepted. Her parents and friends didn't feel this way. They just knew that Tiffany, in doing her best, would do an outstanding job.

Tiffany's desire for acceptance resulted in pathological behavior. Knowing she wasn't perfect and feeling somewhat unworthy of unconditional acceptance, she began to seek acceptance by giving to others. In his classic *Four Loves,* C. S. Lewis calls this "gift love." Her behavior led Tiffany to choose boyfriends whom she could help. Her parents and friends couldn't understand Tiffany. There were many talented boys on campus, yet she chose to date and eventually marry someone who was not as social, intellectual or spiritual as she. Tiffany had her reasons, though. This guy needed her and she didn't have to worry about feeling guilty if she wasn't perfect because it didn't matter to him. It was a comfortable relationship and highly satisfying emotionally.

He became dependent on her to gain him social acceptance, to help him academically, to write potential graduate schools and to fill out job applications. He didn't perceive any need to have her help him spiritually, although that need was what first drew her to him. He had a very shallow experience with the Lord, and Tiffany had just come back from a summer mission experience overseas and was bubbling over with enthusiasm. When his interest in being helped spiritually was not appreciated, she went overboard in the other areas, even causing her own grades and social activities to suffer. And because he didn't appreciate her spiritual fervor, that aspect of her life slowly was neglected.

Because of the mutual dependency in this relationship, it felt satisfying to both. They needed each other—and they considered themselves the perfect match.

But shortly after marriage the illusion began to fade. Tiffany realized her husband wasn't perfect. In fact, he had a long way to go. Immediately she put him on a self-improvement course so he would become the perfect husband. He didn't take that for long. As he began to resent her help, she turned her attentions to others who were in need and appeared far more accepting.

As a perfectionist, Tiffany never felt worthy of acceptance unless she was giving "gift love" to others. This giving, however, caused feelings of emotional dependency in relationships outside their marriage. Only Tiffany's strong moral code kept her from becoming physically involved. These relationships usually lasted as long as the other person would accept Tiffany's "gift love." Tiffany never saw any danger, but these relationships nearly destroyed her marriage.

The crisis came when one relationship lasted so long that emotional dependency turned into feelings of love. Physical intimacy began to be desired by both parties. Tiffany was living in an illusion that this was the perfect relationship, only her moral standards wouldn't allow her to give herself sexually to someone other than her husband.

When she began to realize that this relationship was more important to her than her relationship with her husband or God, she became frightened and sought help. Through counseling, she and her husband were able to understand the pathological dynamics that were happening in their marriage and Tiffany began to work on overcoming her perfectionistic personality. They're still together, but it's been a rocky road.

If only Tiffany (and probably her husband) hadn't brought emotional hang-ups into their marriage. If only these hidden agendas could have been discovered before marriage, I wonder if they would have chosen to marry each other?

A wise mate faces the pathology of his or her past and deals with it before marriage, regardless of the time it takes or the cost involved.

Making Mature Decisions

Decisions are personal choices based on values and needs. Two people could make completely opposite choices, and yet both would be making a decision that is good for them.

Mature decisions result when individuals deny immediate self-gratification and consider carefully all the options. The problems begin when impulsive decisions are made without gathering the necessary information to make a responsible choice.

Let's say you want to purchase a car. What do you need to know in order to make a good decision?

- Is this the best car for the money?

- Do you have enough money to purchase it?

- Do you really need a car right now?

- How much is the insurance?

- Is this the best time to purchase the car?

- What impact will this car have on your current life? (In other words, what will you have to give up in order to have enough money for its purchase?)

One engaged young man purchased a car that put him $8,000 in debt. In all honesty, he didn't need the car for another six months, and by then the next year's models would be available. Still, he purchased the car based on assumptions that turned out to be false. He assumed he would get a fulltime, good-paying job right out of college. He didn't. In turn, he didn't have enough money for the insurance, so he stored the depreciating car in a garage. When he did get a job, he had to work weekends to keep up the car payments. He and his fiance no longer had all the special time they used to enjoy together.

Before his car was even out of storage, another assumption proved false. He had assumed his fiance would get a job during their first year of marriage so they could make car payments and he could go to graduate school. Now, she was considering graduate school too. Would the purchase of this car rob him of attending graduate school and affect his career? He began to wonder if the car was worth it.

Mature decision makers aren't afraid to seek—and take—advice from those who are more experienced. Mature decision makers won't make a decision until all the information is in and the consequences are carefully weighed. Mature decision makers aren't impulsive decision makers.

In no area is mature decision making more important than in the area of finances. A few bad choices can put a newly married couple in debt for a lifetime, destroying their aspirations. For example, because of financial obligations a couple may have to work longer hours, leaving them without time or money for the vacations they had wanted to take. Their debt is like a wet blanket dampening their dreams.

To determine if you are making wise and mature decisions, ask yourself these questions:

1. *Am I willing to deny immediate gratification for long-term life goals?*

2. *Am I living a balanced life?*

All work and no play isn't good for your health — and can destroy a marriage. Begin living a balanced life spiritually, socially, intellectually and physically before marriage and it's easier to maintain one afterwards.

3. *Am I clear on my life goals? Do I know where I want to go in life?*

Finding yourself and getting the education you need will make you a much more desirable marriage partner. Without the burden of trying to combine school and a job, you will be able to concentrate on your spouse and your relationship even more.

4. *Have I established trustworthy friendships with people who have a positive influence on me?*

It isn't healthy to have all your emotional needs met in the person you marry. Friends enrich a marriage. Before marriage, cultivate friendships with others. They can provide social stimulation that is healthy for a marriage.

If your "friends" make you feel inadequate, or tempt you to participate in things you know you shouldn't, re-evaluate. You don't need them. Remember this helpful motto: "Be a friend and you will find a good friend."

Develop Your Spiritual Life

There is nothing as important as a personal relationship with the Lord to get you through the difficulties that all couples experience. Although a dynamic relationship with God is not a panacea, it sure helps. When you and your spouse can pray together, share Bible promises and seek the way you should go based on biblical principles, you have a major advantage over couples who don't. Your chances of ultimately experiencing a lifelong marriage of happiness and fulfillment are significantly greater.

Consider a married couple I read about. They had been separated for more than a year when they gave their hearts to the Lord and decided to try living together again. They agreed to no longer trust themselves for solutions to their problems. Instead, they went together to the Lord and had what they called a "white knuckle" prayer. They would grasp each other's hands, interlock their fingers and begin to pray. "Lord," Joe would say, "You know I can't stand it when Mary starts to nag. But Lord, You can take anything. Help me react as You would react. And Lord, if You could change Mary just a little, I'd sure appreciate it." And then Mary would pray a similar prayer: "Lord, I can't stand it when Joe tells me he is going to do something and he doesn't. Give me Your patience. But if You could also help Joe to be a little more responsible, I'd be thankful."

How did prayer solve their problems? First of all, it allowed time for tempers to cool so Joe and Mary could think more clearly. Second, prayer helped Joe and Mary be open to the Holy Spirit's influence. At that point they were more willing to compromise or look for creative answers to formerly unsolvable conflicts.

It's also healthy to learn to share your negative feelings with the Lord rather than hurt your loved one.

For example, wives sometimes irrationally feel neglected. Let's say your husband faithfully takes you out for a dinner date each week. One week he misses the date because of a business meeting which may ultimately mean an advancement in his career. You shouldn't feel neglected, but you do. How should you respond? Give your feelings to the Lord. Say, "Lord, I'm feeling neglected, but I know it's not true. Help me overcome these feelings and replace them with something positive. Help me find the promise I need in Your Word that will make me feel good once again."

It works. It really does. And how fortunate it is when you have developed this close relationship with the Lord *before* marriage. A Spirit-filled life produces love, joy, peace, long-suffering, kindness, goodness, faithfulness, gentleness and self-control. It's qualities like these that make a great mate.

Valuing and accepting yourself, dealing with the pathology of your past, making mature decisions, and developing your spiritual life are only a few of the ingredients that make a great mate. But once you've conquered these, the rest should be easy. And someday, some special person is going to be mighty lucky to win your love.

❤ ❤ ❤

Something to Think About . . .

Of the four qualities that make a great mate mentioned in this chapter, which is your strongest area? Which is your weakest? Write down three things you will do this month to strengthen your weak area.

Tangling With
the Temperaments

Faye loves people. She is talkative and vivacious—the life of the party. Bob's friends envy him living with such a happy, spontaneous wife. But Bob doesn't think he is so lucky. Faye's forgetfulness and disorganization bug him. Why can't she just put her keys or glasses in one place so she can find them? And she is always missing appointments because she forgets to look at her calendar—that's if she has remembered to write it on the calendar in the first place.

Faye's feelings about Bob? She considers her perfectionistic husband an old "stick-in-the-mud." He never has any fun. He is always picking things up, putting things away, filing, making lists and methodically checking off each item. And no matter how much Faye teases and begs, he won't budge from his easy chair if it's his scheduled reading time. He is so organized—and so boring!

What's the problem in this marriage? Tangled temperaments!

Doris is a dynamite go-getter. She is a sharp real estate agent who was promoted to branch manager before the end of her first year on the job. She has a special knack to see what needs to be done and has no trouble telling others what to do. This habit, however, spills over into her home life, and she ends up being a nagging wife.

But what else would you expect if you were married to Stanton? He never does anything! He just sits there watching TV. Nothing would ever get done around the home if it weren't for Doris, or so she thought. Stanton is easygoing and enjoys a good time. And the more Doris nags, the more Stanton retreats and stubbornly does what he wants to do without informing his wife.

What went wrong in this relationship? Tangled temperaments!

What could help Faye and Bob, Doris and Stanton? An understanding of the temperaments. A temperament is a natural disposition. It's an inborn behavioral style that permanently affects your manner of thinking, feeling and acting—and it is reflected in your personality. Understanding the differences between the temperaments while you are still in the dating stage can save you from a mountain of adjustment problems during those first few years of marriage.

Can Temperaments Change?

Unlike interests, your temperament seldom, if ever, changes. Change in behavior, of course, is always possible. This may make it appear that a person's basic temperament has changed, but this is probably not so.

For example, let's take "forgetful" Faye. Faye may come to the realization that her forgetfulness is getting in the way of a positive relationship with her husband. An irresponsible reaction would be to lament, "Well, that's just the way I am. Take me or leave me!" Too often, that's exactly what happens. The spouse either resentfully chooses to remain married, or decides it isn't worth it and leaves.

How much better it would be if Faye would choose to change her behavior. Realizing that she is not naturally organized and has a problem remembering things, Faye decides to purchase a large calendar and she hangs it next to the telephone. Every message is then written on that calendar. She also carries with her an appointment book which she updates every morning before leaving the house. She makes a list of things she must do that day—items that need to be purchased and appointments that need to be kept. She also organizes her home so everything has a place, including her keys and glasses, and then she works hard to always put them there. Forgetfulness is still a natural part of her temperament, but she is not going to let it destroy her marriage.

Does "boring" Bob have any responsibility to change? Of course he does. He can choose to deviate from his schedule when he realizes it would make Faye happy. Why not leave the mowing of the lawn one more day in order to take advantage of a seminar Faye would like to have him attend with her? It doesn't change his basic temperament, but his flexible behavior is a lot more fun to live with.

And what about Stanton and Doris? If Stanton continues to follow his natural inclination to take life easy and put things off until he feels like doing them, his temperament may cost him his marriage. Realizing that Doris is a natural boss who ends up nagging if things don't get done, Stanton has gotten in the habit of asking Doris every morning what she would like him to do that day. Together they go over the list of suggestions and decide on the feasibility of accomplishing these things in the next twenty-four hours. If there is a special on TV that evening, it is planned into their schedule so Stanton doesn't have to listen to Doris's nagging and feel guilty because he has chosen to watch it.

And what about Doris's nagging? Well, she knows that it comes naturally for her to tell others what to do, but she doesn't want to be a nag. Since, however, it is a long-term habit, she's going to need some help to change. She has asked Stanton to let her know when she starts nagging. All he has to say in a genuinely empathetic way is, "Sweetheart," and she gets the message and chooses to change her behavior.

Unless they are understood, accepted and appreciated, temperaments can become tangled and strangle the life out of a marriage. And you'll find that very few couples are like Bob and Faye and Doris and Stanton. Not too many people modify their behavior *after* marriage. That's why it is important during the dating process to understand your own temperament and that of the person you love. Discuss your unique temperaments—and what bugs you about the other. If one person becomes defensive or is unwilling to discuss these differences, you shouldn't consider marriage yet.

If you truly love each other, you will want to work on some behavioral changes that might make your relationship more satisfying and increase your chances for a fulfilling marriage. Determine together what changes you each would like to make and then keep your relationship on a dating basis long enough to see if these changes in behavior become permanent. If you are both comfortable with the persons you have become, you may be ready to consider engagement.

Just remember, it's only the behavior that has changed. Your basic temperaments have remained the same. Unless you can truly respect each other's basic temperaments, don't get married. These temperaments will continue to be exhibited throughout life in ways you can't even imagine right now. Even though changes seem to have been made during your courtship, there is no guarantee that they will continue to be made or that your partner won't revert to old habit patterns after marriage.

How Knowing the Temperaments Can Help

The theory of temperaments is ancient. Hippocrates, who lived hundreds of years before Christ, was the first to write about temperaments and to make an effort to categorize them in some way. He observed four significantly different types of individuals with clusters of related behaviors. He named these temperament styles after different body fluids: sanguine (the happy, pleasure-loving person) was the Greek word for blood; choleric (the strong-willed and sometimes angry controller) for "yellow bile"; melancholy (the sensitive perfectionist that has a tendency toward sadness and depression) for "black bile"; and phlegmatic (the easygoing, peace-loving and sometimes indifferent individual) for phlegm.

When I first studied these temperaments, I was amazed to find that some psychologists still refer to such ancient thinking today. Also, I had a very difficult time accepting the idea that people could be put into boxes. Human behavior is much more complex than that. God's creativity is such that there has never been two individuals who were exactly the same—not even identical twins. How could man be so bold as to attempt to put a person's personality in a box?

Years later, my fourteen-year-old son, Kevin, and I were listening to some seminar tapes on the four temperaments. As Kevin listened to the description of the choleric person, he insightfully commented, "Mom, she's talking about Dad." I had to agree; the description of the choleric person, who sees what needs to be done and tells people what to do, did sound like the administrator I married. We laughed and I thought that was the end of it.

The next day, however, when choleric Dad came home from work, he greeted his phlegmatic son in his typical way, "Hi, Kev. Have you fed the dogs yet?" Kevin, who usually resented his dad's reminders, came running to me with a big smile on his face, saying, "Hey, Mom, there's my choleric dad again!" Kevin's insight about his father's temperament helped him respect his dad for the way he was, rather than resent him because he wasn't as easygoing as his son.

Suddenly, I realized there might be something positive about this simplistic way of categorizing people. If a person could use this tool to better understand himself and the person he lives with, perhaps he could accept his mate's personality and behavior patterns easier. A person might also understand better how he himself could change in order to foster a more satisfying marriage relationship. And the earlier in a relationship a person gets this understanding, the better.

Opposites Attract

Understanding temperaments can be a helpful tool in the selection of a life partner. I'm sure you know by now that opposites attract—but opposites don't necessarily have an easy time living together. If you know (or suspect) that you and the person you're serious about are opposites in personality, there are a few things you can do to tame the sparks that are sure to fly between you.

First of all, accept the fact that you're opposites. You can have a dynamic, exciting, passionate marriage and be totally opposite in temperaments—*if you truly respect each other.* If you love each other, you will never try to make the other change to do things the "right" way—the way you think things should be done. Opposites must give freedom to their loved one, allowing him or her to express himself in the way most comfortable to him.

Second, if you're opposites, be prepared to work harder to make sure your marriage doesn't become trapped in a mire of misunderstanding and resentment about your differences. This may mean dialoging each day about your growing relationship, or reading books about communication and problem solving and putting the techniques you learn into practice. You may need to take marriage enrichment courses together, or even go for professional counseling if the going gets rough.

When I started writing this book, a friend came up to me and said, "Make sure you tell young lovers how difficult the first year of marriage is."

"What do you mean?" I asked.

"Well," my friend replied, "there are just so many adjustments you have to make in getting used to another person."

I thought about that statement. Of course, there are always adjustments to make in marriage. But it doesn't have to be difficult. No doubt, the more similar two people are, the more they can understand each other. Usually that means less adjusting to each other once they're married. But opposites can learn to adjust as well. They'll just have to work at it a little more.

You make the choice. At least during these dating years, you can make a more informed choice by understanding the strengths and weaknesses of each other's temperaments and how one type of temperament might affect another. We'll spend the rest of the chapter looking at the dynamics of temperaments in a relationship.

Defining the Temperaments

Let's go back to Hippocrates and take a look at the four basic temperaments he described. As you read, remember that there is no such thing as a pure sanguine, choleric, melancholy or phlegmatic person, so don't be concerned if you can't find yourself clearly in one category. We are all shades and blends of the various temperaments. The important thing to consider is the weaknesses in each of these temperaments, and work on overcoming these.

One more caution. Don't pigeonhole yourself in one of these categories and then use your natural temperament as an excuse for your behavior. *You control your behavior.* You don't have to be a slave to your temperament. You can change.

Sanguine

Sanguines like to be the center of attention and have a good time. They do things for pleasure. Most sanguines are outgoing, talkative, friendly, optimistic, enthusiastic, cheerful, spontaneous, creative, sincere and curious. They also have a sense of humor, are childlike, somewhat forgetful, impulsive, and often controlled by circumstances, which may cause them to be irresponsible at times. They may get angry easily, but they don't usually hold grudges. They are the life of the party and enjoy being up front. They volunteer for jobs, spontaneously touch and inspire others, and are, in short, people-oriented. But their relationships may be based on a selfish motive, since sanguines crave an audience.

If you find yourself in this category, you may need to make the effort to think of others before yourself. Try making people feel special by remembering their names and birthdays, and by taking the time to really listen to others rather than doing all the talking yourself.

When you enthusiastically volunteer your time and talents, be sure you carry your fair share of responsibility. And stick to a project until it's finished — even though it may no longer be much fun. Learn to delegate when appropriate.

You may also need to start planning more so you will be better prepared for future events. If you spend a little more time getting organized and pay more attention to details, those around you will be happier.

Choleric

Cholerics are goal- or product-oriented, and they enjoy getting things done. It's not hard for cholerics to become workaholics. They are natural leaders, and are good at delegating work and motivating others. Cholerics are usually well-organized, confident, dynamic, active, strong-willed, independent, not easily discouraged, practical, impatient, unemotional and, at times, bossy and controlling. The problem is, they are probably right! Cholerics enjoy controversy and seem to have little need for friends. They see in terms of the big picture and can figure out quickly what needs to be done. That's why they excel in emergencies.

If you are a choleric, you may need to make some changes that will make you easier to live with. Accept the fact that no one is perfect. Don't pressure others into your "high-performance" standard. Be willing to apologize and say, "I'm sorry," when you're wrong.

Learn to relax. Take time to make friends and to participate in fun activities. Cultivate patience by not expecting immediate solutions to everything. Encourage others' ideas and choices rather than constantly forcing your own.

Melancholy

Are you a deep thinker? Do you have a perfectionistic bent? Are you deeply sensitive? Then you're probably a melancholy. Here's the textbook description of a melancholy: analytical, conscientious, idealistic, artistic, enjoys details and beautiful things. Melancholies are economical and self-sacrificing. Because they take things seriously, they are easily depressed, pessimistic, suspicious of others and often moved to tears. They avoid attracting attention and are content to stay in the background. Melancholy people may be cautious when making friends, but they are devoted once they're in a relationship. They make good listeners and great helpers.

My advice to the melancholies: Learn to enjoy every day. Try to be more spontaneous and do things that are pleasurable. Take the time to cultivate and enjoy more friendships.

Because melancholies have a tendency toward negative thinking, they must work on thinking positively. They need to work on counting their blessings and expressing thanks, while resisting the temptation to gossip and spread bad news. And because melancholies are usually perfectionists, they must make a concerted effort to accept themselves and others unconditionally.

Phlegmatic

The phlegmatic person is the peace-loving, conflict-avoiding observer. Other traits might include: easygoing, relaxed, calm, patient, sympathetic, kind, compassionate, competent, steady, agreeable, not easily upset, quiet, observant and inoffensive. Phlegmatics dislike change. They tend to keep their emotions to themselves and are good under pressure. They are easy to get along with, and because they take time to talk and listen, they usually have many friends.

If you are phlegmatic, you need to know that your laid-back attitude is often a source of irritation to others. You've got to learn to pull your fair share. Be observant about what needs to be done and don't put off doing it. Solve problems when they arise. Learn to talk through difficult situations rather than retreat from them. Share negative feelings instead of bottling them up. Show motivation and enthusiasm. Don't be afraid to try new things. Laugh, smile and express positive emotion on a regular basis.

When the Temperaments Tangle

Have you found the one or two temperaments that sound like you? How about the person you're seriously dating? What is he or she like?

Now we'll take a look at what the potential problems might be if you were to marry someone of a different temperament. While none of these problems is insurmountable, you'll do yourselves a favor to talk about your personality differences before you make a lifetime commitment.

The sanguine and the choleric: The sanguine wants to have a good time while the choleric wants to get things done. The sanguine is impulsive, childlike and forgetful while the choleric is organized, practical and bossy. Can you see areas of possible conflict?

The sanguine and the melancholy: The sanguine says, "If we've got to do it, let's have fun!" The melancholy says, "If we do it, then let's do it right." They approach life from opposite ends of the spectrum which, ultimately, is the source of most of their conflicts.

The sanguine and the phlegmatic: The sanguine is

impulsive and outgoing. The phlegmatic doesn't like to try new things and may be a bit introverted. And while the sanguine is talkative and willing to share feelings, the phlegmatic prefers to bottle up negative feelings and avoid problem-solving. These differences can easily cause misunderstandings.

The choleric and the melancholy: Because they both like to see things get done, the choleric and the melancholy may be more alike than some of the other temperaments. But they can tangle if the choleric is interested in the practical way to get something done immediately, and the melancholy insists on perfection regardless of how long it takes.

The choleric and the phlegmatic: Here is a real potential for conflict. The choleric is a doer; the phlegmatic is not. The choleric leaves the house in the morning expecting that certain things will be accomplished by the phlegmatic. The phlegmatic happily spends his or her day on other pursuits—and never quite gets around to the choleric's "To Do" list. Too often this leads to nagging, bossy behavior from the choleric. The phlegmatic isn't as open about feelings and so tries to avoid conflict by not saying anything. Over the years internal resentment begins to build and before the choleric/phlegmatic couple realizes it, the phlegmatic's affection has turned to hostility. Once this happens, it is very difficult to restore the original love relationship.

And look out when the wife is a choleric who naturally assumes a leadership position while the husband feels that even though he is a phlegmatic, he should be the head of the household. This couple is heading for rough waters.

Mutual respect is the stuff that holds a choleric/phlegmatic marriage together. Without it, a couple is doomed to a relationship gone cold due to harbored resentment and anger.

The melancholy and the phlegmatic: While melancholies and phlegmatics both have more introverted personalities, there are some basic differences. First of all, their attitudes may conflict. The phlegmatic is usually more positive, and the melancholy tends to be a pessimist.

Another conflict might arise in regards to how things are done. The melancholy is extremely conscientious, paying attention to details and making sure things are done right. The phlegmatic couldn't care less. Can you see the melancholy partner following around the phlegmatic, picking up after him and retouching projects that the phlegmatic considered done? I can almost hear the melancholy complain, "Can't you ever do anything right?" And if you listen carefully, you could hear the phlegmatic lament, "Why can't you just accept me the way I am?"

Marrying someone with a different temperament can make life interesting. Just make sure you date each other over a long enough period of time, and see each other in as many different situations as possible, so you have a pretty good idea about how your temperaments mesh, and then you can accept and respect those differences.

When Jan and I got married, I was ignorant of our different temperaments and how they might affect our relationship. I did know he was very methodical, organized and wouldn't think of starting his day without a list. In my book, lists were for letting people know what you wanted for Christmas, not for organization!

After marriage we got along just fine as long as he didn't *tell* his impulsive, disorganized and fun-loving wife what to do. In fact, our differences in temperaments didn't really tangle until the children came along. I felt Jan unfairly blamed me when I didn't make the children do everything he had listed for them to do.

I resented him for being too hard on the kids and then punishing me for their disobedience. *After all,* I thought, *if he asked them to do something, it was his responsibility to make sure they did it, not mine.*

The crisis came one Friday night. I had been blamed one time too many, and he was utterly frustrated with the wife he couldn't control. I stood up and said, "Enough. I'd rather live alone than be constantly blamed for something that wasn't my fault and manipulated by your anger." He was shocked. He had no idea I felt so strongly about it, and he certainly hadn't meant to hurt me. He was only doing what he felt was necessary to keep his family organized and help his wife be a better mother.

That night was a major turning point in our acceptance of each other's differences. By openly sharing how deeply we felt, we gained a better understanding of why we did the things we did. The result? Our respect for each other deepened and our expectations became more realistic.

You can't avoid all the temperament tangles in marriage, but the more you can grow to accept and respect each other's differences before marriage, the fewer tangles there will be after.

❤   ❤   ❤

Something to Think About . . .

What temperament category do you find yourself in? What about the person you're dating? Make a list of ways in which you find your personalities compatible. Now list the areas of potential conflict. Do your areas of conflict outweigh the areas of compatibility? How will you use your understanding of the temperaments to help diffuse your next argument?

♥ 7 ♥

Enjoying the Single Life

I vividly remember my college days and the frustration of liking guys who never glanced my way, the awkwardness of tactfully trying to get out of dates with guys who wouldn't take no for an answer—and the agony of waiting. Waiting for a phone call for a Saturday evening date (it didn't come). Waiting for that handsome man to walk me to class (he walked my best friend instead).

Even after I was married I had recurring nightmares of not dating, or of watching the man with whom I was madly in love pay fond attention to someone else. This may not sound like the subject matter of most nightmares, but I assure you these dreams were every bit as terrifying. I experienced heart-wrenching agony because I was not able to catch the man of my dreams.

If it weren't for those recurring nightmares, I might have forgotten the fear of rejection that is often part of the dating years. For many it is agony. But rest assured, you are not the only one who has suffered. The fear of not being able to find the right marriage partner is a common one. And not even popularity, good looks or money can shield you from these feelings. However, don't let those feelings ruin this special time in your life.

Being single can hold unique opportunities. You may even find that once you get involved doing what you've always had a desire to do, you actually *enjoy* your single status. And in the process you'll meet some fascinating people and you'll give yourself the chance to meet the right person for you. Here's some ideas on how to make the best use of this time in your life.

Get Involved in Group Activities

Avoid becoming a recluse. Don't talk yourself into staying home, convincing yourself that you would rather read a good book than be out doing something with someone else. Make yourself sign up for the beach party, cheer for your school's team, join the choir or become a member of the ski club.

Join a singles' group. This is a great way to get acquainted with interesting people. If your church doesn't have a singles' group, why not start one? Or you may want to check into other churches in your community and join an established group.

I admit it's not always easy getting involved in group activities, especially when you think everyone else in the group has a special friend and you don't. But if you'll crank up your self-worth and get involved, you'll soon find that there are quite a number of singles searching for friends who are also frightened of being alone in a group.

Cultivate Friendships

Every friendship (both male and female) adds something to your growth and personal under-standing. Great marriage partners usually have a wide variety of friends who have taught them a lot about the importance of sharing interests, developing new skills, getting along with different personalities, communicating feelings and needs, and unselfishly giving up time and attention to others—all important lessons that prepare a person for marriage.

However, don't limit yourself by thinking every friend has to be marriage material. In fact, not every person you may go someplace with has to be screened for mate potential. Casual "dating" is an important way to cultivate friendships of all types—and an important precursor to more serious dating. Perhaps it should be called "appointment-making" rather than dating. After all, you don't consider it a "date" when you call someone and say, "Hey, haven't seen you in a long time. What about lunch?" I believe marriages would be happier if more of this type of friendship cultivation went on prior to serious dating.

Too many young people miss so much in life because they are afraid to cultivate various types of friendships. They are so busy hunting for their one and only that they miss the blessings of good friends along the way.

Say Yes

Craig was one of the most popular guys on campus. The Sadie Hawkins banquet was coming up where girls asked guys, and Craig thought Sheila might ask him. She was popular and talented, and they had a good time joking together in chemistry lab.

One day, however, as Craig walked out of the cafeteria, he heard a faint voice behind him. It was Rhoda. "Craig, ah, I mean," Rhoda stammered, "I was wondering if you'd go to the banquet with me."

Rhoda was not Craig's type. Other than attend class, she didn't participate in school activities. She was shy. Her straight brown hair, plain features and sometimes unkempt appearance did not make her especially appealing.

"Well, I don't know, Rhoda," he hesitated. "You caught me by surprise. I really don't know . . . "

Craig saw a look of disappointment cross Rhoda's face. How could he do this to her? It must have taken a lot of courage for Rhoda to ask him. Why shouldn't he go with her? He had no real reason to say no, other than his own selfish desire. But he had two big reasons to say yes. It would make Rhoda happy, and she had asked him first.

"Rhoda," he said at last, "I'd be happy to go."

His buddies couldn't believe it. When they started to tease, he cut them short. He wouldn't allow Rhoda to be demeaned. On the night of the banquet Rhoda looked lovely, especially with the beautiful corsage Craig had given her. She held her head high and smiled. They had a good time getting acquainted. Though they never dated again, each gained a new friend that evening.

When I first heard this story, I thought that's probably what Christ would have done. In fact, Jesus attended a banquet where a woman with a questionable reputation, a former prostitute, wanted to anoint Him with perfume. He could have easily pushed her away, like Simon wanted Him to do, but Christ thought more of the feelings of others than about His own feelings and reputation. He allowed this woman to show her appreciation in this way rather than embarrassing her by refusing her attentions. Why not follow Christ's example and say yes to an "appointment" to make someone happy?

"But if I say yes once," I can hear you saying, "won't the person keep bugging me to say yes again?" Not if you make it clear that you want to be a friend, not a date.

Enjoy Being Single

A great way to scare off even a highly interested suitor is to make it known that you are desperate to get married. Too many single people waste what should be the best years of their lives plotting and planning how they can snag the best marriage partner. Then they spend the next half a century singing this jingle:

I wish I were single again, again.
I wish I were single again.
For if I were single, my pockets would jingle.
I wish I were single again.

I married a wife, Oh then, Oh then,
I married a wife, Oh then,
She beat me; she banged me;
    she vowed she would hang me.
I wish I were single again.

My wife, she died, Oh then, Oh then,
My wife she died, Oh then,
My wife she died, I laughed till I cried,
For now I was single again.

I married another, Oh then, Oh then,
I married another, Oh then,
I married another, was worse than the other,
I wish I were single again.

Marriage will come in God's time. Listen to those who have traveled this road before and they will tell you it is far better being single than being married to the wrong person.

So enjoy yourself. Take every day as it comes along and make the most of it as you cultivate your own skills and interests. You'll be a much more desirable date if you approach life with this attitude—and a much, much more desirable mate.

Serve Others

The worst thing you can do while you're single is to feel sorry for yourself. Avoid thoughts of self-pity by reaching outside yourself and serving others. Your problems will seem small, indeed, when you start getting involved with others—especially those who really need you.

Have you ever considered mission service? There are hundreds of exotic places (and some not so exotic) that could benefit greatly by your willingness to serve. Kim, my daughter, spent a summer in Paris volunteering at the Country Life Restaurant, a Christian witnessing program in the heart of the city. You might prefer working with an agricultural project in Africa, building a church school in Palau, or sailing with a mission boat which provides medical care to the people of the Marshall Islands.

If you don't like to travel, there are many closer-to-home places to serve. What about the local day-care center, hospital, nursing home, hospice, library, non-profit ministry, or Christian radio station? And there are hundreds of volunteer jobs just waiting to be filled in local churches.

When you get involved serving others, a wonderful thing happens—you forget about yourself. Plus, you meet some very interesting people in some of the most unlikely places.

Do the Things You Have Always Wanted to Do

Too many people get married thinking that marriage will automatically fill their cup of unfulfilled dreams to overflowing. That seldom happens.

Use the time that you're single to do the things you have always wanted to do. There are many things that may be much easier to do now than after you've made a commitment to someone else.

Have you ever wanted to travel? Do it. There are many young adults who travel in small groups and camp throughout Europe, sail the Caribbean, travel the Orient, or join an archeological dig in the Middle East. If this is your dream, begin talking about it with your friends, read everything you can find about it in the library, call a travel agency or check the colleges and universities and ask about their summer tour programs and their field study courses.

One Christmas when we were camping in the Virgin Islands, a group of students from Michigan State University were there studying ecology. And my daughter took advantage of a summer tour to Europe and received twelve units of credit from her university.

Where there is a will, there is a way. Now is the time to make your dreams come true. And what a much more interesting person you will be to your friends in the future because of your travel experiences.

Have you ever wanted to get another degree? Don't wait. My heart goes out to young couples who marry before they finish their educations. When one or both are trying to juggle night classes, a job and a family, it's a wonder they can maintain their sanity. And if kids happen along unexpectedly, they might as well try climbing Mt. Everest in a wheelchair. Right now, while you are single, may be your window of opportunity to complete the education you desire. Go for it!

Start a Self-improvement Course

No one is so beautiful, talented, intelligent or polite that he or she couldn't benefit by a self-improvement course. Assess yourself. What could you do to improve yourself? It may help to talk to your best friends or a trusted teacher or counselor and get their input.

Do you want to make a change in your physical appearance? Have a color analysis done to determine what colors look best on you. Get your hair styled. Join an exercise class and tone up your muscles. Lose weight — or gain it. Go shopping with someone who can help you select a couple of outfits that make you look your best. If there is something you really don't like about your appearance and it can be changed, change it. It's never too late to get those crooked teeth straightened, or to have plastic surgery, if you feel this would make you happier.

Just remember that what you are in your heart is ultimately more important than how you look. If your "insides" are attractive, they'll add a beauty to your physical appearance that can't be matched by any improvement you do on the outside.

Are you looking for ways to improve your personality? Dale Carnegie's classic, *How to Win Friends and Influence People*, is a good beginning. And while you are at it, why don't you pick up a good etiquette book? Social know-how will help you feel more comfortable in various group situations. Take the time to learn how to be a great conversationalist. Develop communication skills that will put others at ease and make them feel they are the most important people in the world. If you can do that for people, they will think you are pretty terrific.

Develop Domestic Skills

Getting married and establishing a home requires the development of certain skills that aren't necessarily taught in school. Bone up on domestic skills now.

Don't make the mistake of equating domestic skills with "woman's work." You may fall in love with a woman who volunteers happily to clean house if you do the cooking and laundry. Or your husband may expect you to help earn the family income while he shares child-rearing responsibilities. More and more couples are finding that stereotyped roles just don't meet their individual needs. Most women today have career training and most men admit they want to be vitally involved in their children's lives. So whether you're male or female, you'll find it to your advantage to develop your domestic skills.

Do you know how to cook creative and nutritious meals? Are you comfortable entertaining guests? A good course in nutrition may be one of the best investments you'll ever make.

Have you had experience doing the laundry, removing spots and ironing shirts? Do you know how to make beds with mitered corners, clean the bathroom tile or shampoo a carpet? And how knowledgeable are you when it comes to the basic maintenance and repair of a car?

Are you comfortable with children? This is an essential skill for both male and female. Start with a good child development course and then supplement your knowledge with real experience. Offer to babysit for friends, or volunteer in the church nursery or a day-care program. You may want to home-school your children someday. Will you be prepared? Perhaps you could volunteer at the local elementary school or take a few education courses.

Do you know how to make and follow a budget? Do you understand your insurance needs and know how to figure your taxes? What about savings and investments?

In time you will need all these skills. Why not get

a head start and learn as much as you can about establishing a home and family now.

Establish a Closer Relationship With Christ

If you're lonely, make Jesus your constant companion. Your dynamic relationship with Him will cushion heartache, rejection and all the other negative emotions you might suffer while you're single.

Lean on His promises. He says that if you will trust in Him, He will give you the desires of your heart (Psalm 37:3,4). I can't think of anything more reassuring than that, can you? Remember, God's timetable is perfect. You don't need to be anxious.

Every minute you invest in developing your relationship with Christ is time well spent. The fruit of the Spirit found in Galatians 5:22 (love, joy, peace, long-suffering, kindness, goodness, faithfulness, gentleness, self-control), which are a byproduct of a dynamic relationship with Jesus, is the best marriage insurance policy you could have.

There are many good Bible studies available to help you mature and grow in the Lord. Visit your local Christian bookstore and look for titles dealing with spiritual leadership, personal discipline, servanthood, love, etc. Through your study you'll discover what makes a good Christian husband and wife.

Finally, memorize Jeremiah 29:11-13:

> For I know the plans I have for you, says the Lord. They are plans for good and not for evil, to give you a future and a hope. In those days when you pray, I will listen. You will find me when you seek me, if you look for me in earnest (TLB).

Avoid the Hazards of the Single Life

With all the joys and opportunities that the single
life holds, there are some dangers to be aware of—especially if your dating life is not turning out exactly as
you planned. When your desires for a home and family
go unfulfilled for a long period of time, you may be
tempted to compromise your standards. I'd like to
encourage you to hold out for God's best, and beware
of the hazards that may cause you to settle for less.

Hazard #1: *You date someone with a questionable
character because you are beginning to lose hope that
the right one will ever appear.*

It's entirely possible that your expectations to find
a perfect mate are unreasonably high and you may
need to readjust your thinking. Marriage means living
with another human being—not an angel. *But,* there
are certain standards you should not compromise just
because you are lonely. For example, do you want to
be married so badly that you're willing to date someone
who has a substance abuse problem, or someone who
promises to make needed changes in his or her life only
to come up with excuses when there are no results?

Only you will be able to decide what ideals you
don't want to compromise. After all, you will be the one
who will have to spend your life living with this person.

Hazard #2: *You are pressured into a sexual
relationship thinking that it will encourage the person
you are dating to make a permanent commitment to you.*

I hope you hear these next three words: It never
works. *IT NEVER WORKS.* Trust me, if the person you
love were willing to make a lifetime commitment, he or
she wouldn't ask for sex outside of that commitment.

Hazard #3: *You rush into a marriage thinking it
may be your last chance.*

Even if you are convinced that you are truly in love

and your boyfriend or girlfriend is everything you want a mate to be, it never pays to rush a good thing. Enjoy each day of your courtship. Make your plans wisely. If it's truly love, and not just passionate desire, it will last. And if you have any doubts about the relationship, that's even more reason to take your time. Too many people who have felt they have waited long enough jump into a marriage and then find themselves wishing they were single again.

The important thing is to enjoy your single life and use this time that God has given you to do what you feel called to do. And who knows who may walk into your life. When you least expect it, a rather ordinary day may become your "enchanted evening."

❤ ❤ ❤

Something to Think About . . .

List the pros and cons of your single status. If you were to stay single for the next few years, what direction would you like your life to take? What would be the first step on that journey? Make a covenant with the Lord now to consistently pray about what He would have you do during this period of your life.

♥ 8 ♥

How to Break Up and Remain Friends

A pilot once turned to his three passengers and announced that the plane's engine had failed and they were going to crash. Their only hope was to bail out, but there were only three parachutes on board and the pilot planned to take one. After the pilot jumped, one of the passengers explained to the other two that he was a famous scientist and considered by some to be one of the brightest men in the world. "I owe it to society," he said, "to take a parachute and jump." And he did, leaving an old man and a Boy Scout.

The old man sadly looked at the youth. "Sonny," he said, "I've lived a good long life. You take that last parachute." Tears came to his eyes.

The Boy Scout replied, "Sir, you don't have to cry. The brightest man in the world just grabbed my knapsack and jumped."

You know what I learned from this story? Don't grab a knapsack when you need a parachute!

No one enters a serious dating relationship anticipating a breakup. You expect fun, companionship and romance. When romance is on the rise, there is an exhilarating feeling that nothing could ever go wrong. But it can. The element of romance seldom lasts forever. In that grey area between romantic illusion and true love, breaking up is a real possibility.

If you're seriously dating, you are at a high risk to suffer the alienation caused by a breakup. When a breakup occurs, you're going to need more than a knapsack to get you safely down from the romantic heights to the solid ground of reality. It's a bitter fall to the depths of rejection.

To make it safely, without incurring psychological scars that may last for months or years, you're going to need a parachute. In fact, you may need more than one. Without them you could find your hopes dashed to pieces, your dreams turned to nightmares and your desires drowned in depression.

Parachute #1: Discover How Dating Behavior Relates to Breaking Up

The first parachute you need is information on how to develop dating relationships in such a way that the risk of breaking up is minimized. The key: Keep the getting-to-know-you period of dating on a friendship level for as long as possible. Once you begin adding the romantic elements of caressing embraces and long, passionate kisses, the danger of suffering the psychological pain of a breakup is significantly increased.

An age-old principle is that the higher you fly, the farther you have to fall and the greater the pain upon impact. As you are building a relationship, it is wise to keep your physical involvement to a minimum through the casual dating stage. When you follow this course, it is relatively easy to move from one relationship to another, making friends, having fun and enjoying the association of a wide variety of individuals, without breaking hearts and crying bitter tears when you move on.

Friends are special commodities. They are what makes life rich and rewarding. The more time you invest in a relationship, the more you experience together, the more you share in common, the greater the chances are that you would enjoy this person's friendship on a long-term basis, regardless of whom you marry. What a shame to feel that you can't continue to be friends with people you once dated just because they weren't right for marriage.

A breakup does not need to signal the end of a friendship. You can break up and still remain good friends if you haven't become too involved physically.

I've often joked that you should never make enemies of old boy- or girlfriends because you never know when you might need them in the future. Case in point: We were fixing the barbed wire fencing around my parents' mountain property in Colorado. The wire suddenly snapped and tore a deep gash in my daughter's boyfriend's finger. I took one look and knew the cut needed stitches. We were miles from an emergency center, and since the young man was from Canada, I didn't know if his insurance would cover the cost of medical care.

I was wondering what to do when I thought of my old boyfriend who was a well-known surgeon with a medical practice about twenty miles away. I called for help, "Don, this is Kay. Would you mind sewing up this guy's finger?" He did it—and without a fee.

Friends are important. Conduct your dating in such a way that the friends you go out with can be kept for a lifetime.

Parachute #2: Avoid Becoming Involved in Relationships You Don't Want to Continue

You make the choice whether a relationship continues. Avoid getting involved with someone who has a negative effect on you. Don't continue dating anyone who puts you down, treats you disrespectfully, or is verbally or physically abusive. Don't kid yourself into thinking this person is the only fish in the sea so you have to put up with hurtful behavior if you want someone to date. Cut off the relationship before you become emotionally attached, saving yourself and the other party a lot of grief.

Also, avoid becoming involved with someone you don't want as a close friend. Don't lead a person on just because you want to be nice and don't know how to turn him or her down gracefully. Learn to say no early in the friendship. It's not fair to play games with another person's emotions just to see what you can get out of the relationship. It's cruel to use people for your own means.

Jane did this. She dated Stan primarily because his folks had money and she enjoyed water skiing and going to their mountain cabin on the weekends. Before she knew it, Stan was madly in love with her and a breakup was inevitable.

Still, just because you don't want to date someone, doesn't mean that person can't be your friend. Many men and women have established quality friendships with each other without pressuring each other into a dating relationship. Unfortunately, some people just can't take no for an answer. There are individuals who are so starved for a friend that the minute anyone shows them any kindness, they immediately think that person is interested in a dating relationship.

The answer isn't to be unfriendly and avoid these

individuals. The answer is to be truthful—*specifically* truthful—about what you want from the relationship. It may not be enough to tell a person starved for a friend, "I just want to be your friend." You may have to say something more specific, "I'd like to be your friend, but nothing more. Please don't call me at home and don't ask me for a date."

If a person does ask you for a date, it's not wrong to say no. Neither is it wrong to go with him or her once, especially when you know it will make the person happy. But be truthful right up front: "I am saying yes because I think we can have a good time together. I am not interested in a dating relationship, so let's just be friends. If you ask me again, I will say no. We don't have to date to be friends."

Parachute #3: Learn to Break Up Gracefully

When you become convinced that a dating relationship is not what you want, you must take the responsibility of ending it. How you do this will either destroy the chances of having this person as a friend in the future, or leave the door of friendship open. Unless the person had a negative influence on your life, you will probably want to maintain his or her friendship. Follow these guidelines for success.

1. Don't lead someone on when you want out.

It is not easy to break up. Some people don't want to hurt the other person so they continue dating, rather than facing the situation. They may even begin treating their date in a negative way, hoping the person will get the hint and want out of the relationship just as badly. Some people, however, never seem to catch on. Sooner or later, you will have to break up. Prolonging the pain by treating the person disrespectfully is a mean thing to do.

2. Be sensitive to the timing of the breakup.

Don't decide to break up on the day your girlfriend flunks her history exam, or on the anniversary of the death of your boyfriend's father. If you know this breakup is going to be emotionally painful for the other person, it might be thoughtful to choose a time when he or she will have other friends available who can be supportive. Although there is never a "good" time for a breakup, use your common sense. Break the bad news gently at the best possible time.

3. Don't say too much.

Be truthful—but not brutally truthful. You don't have to try and justify why you want to break up by giving a speech on "100 Reasons I Don't Want to Date You Anymore." Many of your reasons may appear shallow to the person being rejected. And it's too easy to get sidetracked and argue over insignificant matters. Just clearly state your reason for wanting to break up in such a way that arguing is unnecessary:

"I am no longer happy in this relationship."

"I feel our differences are too great to have a lasting relationship."

"I have a desire to date other people."

"I feel I am too immature to settle down into a steady relationship."

Note: Each one of these reasons started with the word "I." That brings me to the next point.

4. Give "I-messages," not "you-messages."

An "I-message" means the sender is taking responsibility for the breakup of the relationship, while a "you-message" casts blame on the other person. Notice the difference between, "*I* am not happy when we are together and *I* often go home feeling hurt," versus, "*You* say things that hurt my feelings."

5. Break up face-to-face.

The breakup will be easier to accept if you at least have the guts to face the person you are breaking up with. Facing the person shows respect. Breaking up over the telephone, where you can discuss the situation together, is the next best way. Avoid a "Dear John" letter, and don't ask someone to do your dirty work for you. Can you imagine how it makes the other person feel when he or she hears about your plans to break up from an acquaintance?

6. Be thoughtful.

It's not a bad idea to cushion your breakup by telling the other person what the relationship has meant to you. Mention a few of the person's admirable traits: "I have really valued our friendship and love your sense of humor. I want to be your friend, but I don't want to continue dating."

Knowing that things are not going well in a relationship can help a person get prepared psychologically for the inevitable. Therefore, it may be thoughtful to warn your steady about a possible breakup. But don't keep threatening and then do nothing about it. No one enjoys a yo-yo existence—up one day and down the next. Be decisive. In the long run it's the least painful way.

If you want to keep a friend but end a dating relationship, be considerate and cushion the blow as much as possible. Remember the Golden Rule to treat others as you would want to be treated.

7. Don't spread gossip and cast blame in order to justify yourself.

The world doesn't need to know all the reasons you chose to end this relationship. Keep negative things to yourself. You don't have to justify your course of action by demeaning the other person. When you are asked about what happened, tell your story in such a way that it casts the best possible light on the person you broke up with. When a former boyfriend or girlfriend learns that you still think he or she is a neat person, it soothes the hurt feelings.

8. Don't avoid each other after a breakup.

When you see your ex, don't look the other way. Wave, say "hi," or stop and say a few words, even if it's about the weather. But be careful not to be so friendly that it gives the other person the message that you are sorry for the breakup and want to get back together again.

At the time of a breakup, the feelings of hurt and rejection may be so strong that you part without having said all that is on your mind. Arranging a time to talk sometime after the breakup can bring the relationship to a more acceptable and satisfying close. This will help salvage the friendship and give you a better understanding of each other.

Even if you are the one breaking up, you may find it difficult seeing your old steady with someone new. But it's going to happen sooner or later, so get ready with a smile and a friendly "hi." It may be an act at first, but you'll find your feelings of attachment fading. Time is a wonderful healer.

Seeing your friend with someone else may cause you to realize just how much you really do care for that person. Carefully sort through your feelings. It may have been a good decision to end the relationship because of your incompatibility, your emotional dependency or the negative influence you were having on each other. The feelings you experience when seeing your ex with someone else may merely be jealousy (someone has moved in on what you had considered your territory) or anger (your friend cared so little for you that he or she could immediately jump into another relationship). Examine your feelings before rushing to the phone and telling your former boyfriend or girlfriend that the breakup was a mistake.

9. Prayer can be a part of a breakup, but don't misuse it.

Avoid "preaching" at the other person or trying to sanctify your actions when you pray. When you say good-bye to a relationship, it is not out of hand to pause and say, "What's happening right now is hurtful to both of us. Let's just ask the Lord to lead us in the way we should go." Ask a special blessing on the person you are breaking up with, that the hurts will heal and God will lead that person to a very special relationship in the future.

Parachute #4: How to React When Someone Breaks Up With You

Now let's turn the tables. You will not always be the one doing the breaking up. What if you don't want a relationship to end but your boyfriend or girlfriend is calling it quits? If you want to save face, heal quickly and hopefully save a friend for the future, here are some important things *not* to do.

1. Don't fall apart.

Instead, take a deep breath. Smile, even though faintly, and calmly say, "I'm sorry you feel this way. I was hoping our relationship could grow into a long-term one. I respect you and your wishes, and I hope we can remain friends. I know God has someone special for both of us and the most important thing is to allow Him to lead us." This speech can blow the other person away—and cement a friendship (not a courting relationship) for life. You don't have to part enemies.

If at the time of the breakup you are too hurt or angry to react calmly, try to avoid saying something you'll regret later. It's better to keep quiet and ask for some time to process what you've heard than to react violently and alienate your friend.

2. Don't do something foolish.

A breakup is not the end of the world, regardless of how you feel. You may feel like quitting your job, flunking out of school, running away, getting drunk or jumping off a cliff. But don't. Your feelings of rejection are temporary. Don't do something impulsive that may alter your life significantly.

Unconsciously you may feel that if you do something traumatic, your old boyfriend or girlfriend will feel sorry for you and come back. This seldom happens. Instead, your foolish actions are a message that you are an unstable person and the breakup was probably a good idea.

3. Don't turn bitter.

The last thing you should do is try and get back at the person who has rejected you with, what I call, psychological murder. Words said at the time of breakup can be deadly. No matter how hurt and angry you may be, if you say hateful things and assassinate your ex's character, it's almost impossible to resurrect a friendship.

Revengeful feelings and actions have a tendency

to boomerang, and you may end up being the person hurt most deeply.

4. Don't beg.

"Oh, John, I just can't live without you. You mean everything to me. Please, let's try again. Please, please, please . . . " That's a great way to drive an even bigger wedge into your friendship. If that's your attitude, your old boyfriend may end up going to great lengths to avoid you and the guilt feelings you have caused him to experience. No matter what you think, you can live without that person. You may be so in love that you don't think you can—*but you can.* Keep telling yourself that.

5. Don't isolate yourself after a breakup.

Rejection makes you want to hide from others who may ask questions or feel sorry for you. But when you're hurting, you *need* friends who will support you. Allow your friends to comfort you and to be a sounding board for your feelings.

While you'll need to spend some time alone to sort out your feelings, just as soon as possible get yourself back into society. Do things you enjoy. Keep busy. Set new life goals and move decisively in that direction. Step out and get involved in helping others. Healing will come much more quickly this way.

6. Don't be ashamed to grieve over your loss.

The more serious your relationship—the more deeply bonded you were to each other—the more painful a breakup will be and the more time you will need to grieve. During this time you may go through four different stages in your grieving process. At first, you may deny that the breakup is actually happening: "He's just infatuated with this other girl and will return to me," or "It's just her time of the month. In a week or so things will be okay."

As it begins to dawn on you that this breakup is real, you may experience anger toward the person who has caused you pain. Here's where you have to guard yourself carefully so you don't do something foolish in an attempt to get back at that person.

In the third stage of grief, you'll feel like blaming yourself for what happened. You'll have a tendency to think, "If only . . . " You may need to discuss your feelings with others so they can help you sort out the reality of the situation from your irrational thoughts. Talk about what you did or didn't do to cause the breakup. Don't blame yourself unnecessarily; this will only add feelings of guilt to your load of grief. This time of reflection can be a learning experience to help you avoid suffering from future rejection.

Finally, grief finishes its work when you realize and accept your breakup. Probably the best thing you can do when the full impact of your loss hits you is to have yourself a good long cry. Sob your heart out. It will really help.

During this grieving period look for comfort in the Scriptures. Start with passages such as Psalm 23, Psalm 27 or Psalm 121. When your life seems darkest, remember these promises: "Weeping may endure for a night, but joy comes in the morning" (Psalm 30:5), or "The Lord is near to those who have a broken heart" (Psalm 34:18).

Afterwards take three deep breaths and a cold shower, get dressed in your favorite outfit, splash on your most expensive cologne, and tackle the world. It's yours.

7. Don't jump immediately into another relationship.

The more serious your relationship was, the more pain the breakup will cause and the more time you will need to heal. Breakup time can be very vulnerable time. Because you are used to being close to another person, you now crave closeness. It's easy to fall into the trap of quickly becoming involved with someone else—anyone else. History is filled with horror stories that are the result of relationships on the rebound. There's enough human misery in the world; you don't have to make a personal contribution.

8. Don't punish yourself.

Rejection causes feelings of self-doubt and sometimes self-hate. Don't fall into the trap of equating your value with whether you can hold a relationship together. Consider how God values you. Because He made you and died for you, you are of supreme value to Him. (Review the Scriptures given in Chapter 6.)

To help you through this period of self-blame, you may have to practice what is called self-talk. Tell yourself all the good things about yourself—and say these things over and over. Don't allow your mind to engage in negative self-criticism. That will just pull you downhill into depression, and the devil will rejoice.

9. Don't begin a smear campaign against the other person.

Avoid treating the person as you think he or she deserves to be treated. Instead, turn the tables and say something kind. Here's some good counsel from Proverbs: "If your enemy is hungry, give him food! If he is thirsty, give him something to drink! This will make him feel ashamed of himself, and God will reward you" (25:21,22, TLB).

Breaking up is hard no matter what side you are on. In most cases, feelings of guilt and sadness accompany this decision. Why not do the unexpected and say something nice about the other person? I have a feeling it will surprise him or her, and you will probably find that your feelings of rejection will heal faster when bathed in a positive spirit.

10. Don't give up God.

Many people testify, especially after a marriage breakup, that the only thing that got them through was their relationship with the Lord. Now is the time to lean on Him. Let His Spirit talk to you and minister to your needs. Search for Bible promises. Memorize them. And when the devil tempts you to become discouraged, fall back on one of God's promises, such as, "Be delighted with the Lord. Then he will give you all your heart's desires" (Psalm 37:4, TLB). It might also help to remember that "all things work together for good to those who love God" (Romans 8:28).

By now you are probably thinking, *I could never react to a breakup in a manner that cool, calm and collected. I could never react with such understanding.* That's because most of us allow our feelings to dictate our actions. Breaking up causes feelings of guilt, alienation, rejection and revenge, and too often without realizing it, actions follow. God's way is the opposite. The apostle Paul says, "So be careful how you act; these are difficult days. Don't be fools; be wise: make the most of every opportunity you have for doing good. Don't act thoughtlessly, but try to find out and do whatever the Lord wants you to" (Ephesians 5:15-17, TLB).

I think this is powerful advice, don't you? It's exactly the parachute you may need someday when you find yourself in a romantic relationship and the engine fails.

❤   ❤   ❤

Something to Think About . . .

How did you handle your last breakup with the person you were dating? What did you do right? What did you do wrong? What did the experience teach you about relationships? What will you do differently in your future relationships because of what you've learned?

• 9 •

Symbol of a Lifetime, One-Flesh Commitment

Trish and Jon are in love. As young adults, they know the difference between infatuation and committed love. Their relationship has weathered some rocky times—and through it all their love continues to grow stronger.

Because both Trish and Jon have plans for graduate study, they realize it may be a few years before they'll be able to marry. But lately they've been feeling some pressure. The hugs are arousing strong responses and the kisses are becoming more intense. They wonder if waiting until marriage for sex is really necessary, or just an old-fashioned concept.

After all, they're totally committed to each other. They're mature, intelligent adults. They know all about safe sex and birth control. And they're planning on being married someday.

Trish and Jon are asking the questions many unmarried couples ask: What's wrong with sexual intercourse before marriage? Is oral sex outside of marriage permissible? How far can we go before we've crossed the line? How can something be wrong when it makes us feel so good?

I know you've asked these questions. These are

legitimate questions, and trite responses aren't going to satisfy. But the answers to these questions won't become clear until you understand why God created sex. (I'll give you a hint—it wasn't just for procreation.)

Why God Created Sex

For all the really important and wonderful things in God's world, He has always had symbols to help us remember certain meanings. For example, after the creation of the world, God gave man the Sabbath to remind him of creation. After the terrifying flood, God gave the rainbow as a symbol of His promise that it would never rain like that again. The sacrificial system was given as a symbol of the terrible consequences of disobedience; the ark of the covenant was a reminder of God's law; baptism was given as a symbol of death to sin and the resurrection to new life . . . The list could go on and on.

"And," I can hear you asking, "what does all this have to do with sex?" Hold on. It's coming.

When Satan wants to diminish the significance of something God designed, his first attack is on the symbol. If he can destroy the symbol, then it's easier for us to forget the real meaning. For example, the rainbow has become a common New Age symbol for the path between man and the master of the universe (Satan). Now that I know this, it's difficult for me to look at the rainbow with the same meaning it held for me as a child.

I know you're still wondering, "What does all this have to do with sex?"

Just this. I believe marriage was God's crowning act of creation. God gave marriage to man to help him comprehend the eternal oneness of the Godhead and to symbolize His relationship to man.

What better symbol could God design for complete unity than sexual intercourse? Two different individuals, a male and a female, joining together in the highest and most intimate form of human love.

That's powerful, and that alone makes the sex act so holy that it becomes difficult to watch movies or listen to music or hear words that attempt to make it commonplace and vulgar.

But there is more. To further symbolize the unchanging unity of the Godhead and God's unchanging relationship to man, marriage should ideally be a lifetime relationship. In order for men and women to be constantly reminded of their commitment to this lifetime unity with their marriage partners, God created sexual intercourse to be so exciting, so pleasurable and so fulfilling that humans would look forward to experiencing it over and over again—each time celebrating and renewing their marital commitment.

Think about it—there is nothing else in the marriage relationship that has this same meaning. Sexual intercourse is the only human act that God reserved exclusively for a marriage partner. And each time this oneness is expressed, each time the exciting climax is reached and each body involuntarily responds to the other, it reminds the couple of the lifetime commitment they have made to each other.

That's why Satan is trying so hard to destroy this symbol. If he can counterfeit sexual intercourse so it no longer symbolizes the unity that God intended, then he has diminished the importance of intercourse as it relates to marriage. And instead of sex turning man's mind to God and His relationship to man, it turns man's mind to self and the fulfillment of his desires. And so far, Satan has been very successful in his quest. In fact, throughout history it is during Satanic orgies that the sexual act becomes the most heinous and degrading sin.

There are at least three ways that Satan has caused sexual intercourse to lose its God-designed meaning of a one-flesh commitment for life:

1. *Sex outside of a marriage commitment.* If you have sexual intercourse outside of a lifetime marriage commitment, it won't hold the same meaning when you are married. In fact, the more people you experience sex with, the less meaningful it becomes. Since there is no other symbol within marriage that says commitment for life, sex in marriage is reduced to merely a pleasurable act rather than something holy.

2. *Sex with the same gender.* If you have "sex" with someone of the same gender—which means oral or anal sex—you destroy its significance. Most homosexual or lesbian relationships aren't stable relationships. Many gays have multiple partners—some have had partners numbering in the thousands. It is impossible for the sex act between two men or two women to have a "one-flesh commitment for life" meaning because their anatomy is the same. A man and a woman's body have been designed by God to fit one inside the other to become one flesh. To have sex with the same gender is counterfeit.

3. *Self-stimulated sexual response.* Masturbation leading to a sexual climax can diminish the true meaning of sexual intercourse as God designed it. And it could possibly affect a future marriage relationship.

I'd like to discuss in more detail Satan's distortion of sex through premarital sex and masturbation, and give you some guidelines to help you set the rules for your own life.

Sex Outside of the Marriage Commitment

Sex outside of marriage diminishes its symbolic meaning of commitment to marriage for life. That is the strongest reason of all to wait. But if you are still asking, "What's wrong with premarital sex?" you might consider these nineteen reasons to wait, any one of which is reason enough to say no.

1. God said so.

Look up the texts for yourself.

- "Now the body is not for sexual immorality but for the Lord" (1 Corinthians 6:13).

- "Flee sexual immorality . . . he who commits sexual immorality sins against his own body. Or do you not know that your body is the temple of the Holy Spirit who is in you, whom you have from God, and you are not your own?" (1 Corinthians 6:18,19)

- "For this is the will of God, your sanctification: that you should abstain from sexual immorality" (1 Thessalonians 4:3).

- "But fornication and all uncleanness or covetousness, let it not even be named among you, as is fitting for saints" (Ephesians 5:3).

And if you're still not convinced, take some time to read the book of Proverbs.

2. Sex before marriage can become a binding force leading to marriage based on sex and not friendship.

Just because you've had sex doesn't mean you should marry a person. This is another falsehood from Satan which will only cause you and the person you marry more misery. You should be responsible for your sexual partner's welfare, but God wants you to marry the person with whom you will have the best possible chance of becoming everything God wants each of you to be.

Perhaps you've already become sexually involved with someone. You can make the choice to stop. Once you understand the true meaning of sexual inter-course, you can choose to be a "virgin" from this day until the day you are married. You will be glad for the choice you've made. God doesn't want a sexual mistake to destroy your life. There will always be consequences for unwise actions, but God forgives, and you can determine to make wise choices from now on.

3. Flashbacks of previous sexual encounters can haunt a marriage.

You can control your body a lot easier than you can control your mind. People who have participated in premarital sex often complain of flashbacks. "It's like having three people making love in one bed," said one man. "Maybe my wife will say something or move in a certain way and before I know it my mind is back on the beach somewhere, or in a van having sex with a girlfriend. I'd give anything to get rid of those memories so I could concentrate on my wife. I really do love her and want to enjoy our marriage relationship to the fullest."

The guilt associated with promiscuous sexual be-havior tends to make flashbacks troublesome.

4. Sex can cover up serious difficulties in a relationship.

"The only time we get along is when we're in bed together," one young woman commented. "When we are away from each other, or together and not making out, it's clear we are so different that we should never get married. But once he starts to kiss me and caress my body, it feels so good that I'm convinced we are made for each other."

5. *Sex can make it difficult to distinguish between real love and infatuation.*

Infatuation is passionate love—feelings generated by biology, not reason. While passionate love is a part of true love, it's not the dominating factor.

It is natural for a married couple to seek privacy to enjoy sexual intimacies. This is part of their need to grow together in unity. However, *before marriage,* one of the major ways to distinguish infatuation from true love is whether the couple is happy only when they are alone with each other. True love draws a couple closer to their families, friends and God. Infatuation causes a couple to pull away from others.

Because sexual intercourse is designed to bring two people together as one, when it is experienced outside of marriage, it can confuse a person's feelings and decision-making ability. Premarital sex feels like it is enhancing oneness and leads a couple to believe it is safe to go ahead and get married. But the fact is, premarital sex usually only promotes body unity and not the mind and soul unity which is necessary for lifetime commitment.

6. *Premarital sex can trigger lifetime guilt and regret.*

It shouldn't, because mistakes happen, but it can. You cannot willfully control every factor of your psychological make-up. Because of being brought up with a strong moral code, or because of one's own moral standards, participation in sexual intercourse before marriage can be more psychologically damaging for some individuals than others. It's best not to take a chance.

Some try to escape guilt feelings by blaming their parents for raising them with such high moral standards. But if these are biblical standards, then that only leads to blaming God—and ultimately suffering more guilt.

It's true—some individuals have hang-ups in regard to sexual behavior which is caused by unhealthy patterning or sexual abuse in childhood. If you perceive this to be a problem in your life, seek a good Christian counselor to help you work through your feelings so you can have the best possible chance for sexual adjustment in marriage.

7. Guilt feelings over sex before marriage can be carried over to sex in marriage.

If you participate in premarital sex and know it's wrong, it's quite natural to feel guilty. The more sex you have will be accompanied by more guilt, and the more difficult it will be later in a marital relationship to have guilt-free sex. Even though you know sex is okay after marriage, your mind still associates it with guilt.

Closely related to this is the way some people train their bodies to respond during sexual excitement. Before marriage, knowing that the act of sexual intercourse is wrong, many couples just pet to the plateau stage of sexual arousal and then back away from each other (which, by the way, is *very* difficult to do). In so doing, they train their bodies to respond only to a certain level and then shut down.

Some individuals who have participated in this practice before marriage find it difficult to achieve the full sexual climax during intercourse because their bodies automatically shut off at a certain point. The next time they have sex with their marriage partner, they are so worried about not achieving a climax that they don't. What happens sexually is pretty well determined by what goes on in your mind—and how you have trained your body.

8. Premarital pregnancy.

If you don't think unintended pregnancy is a problem today, just look at the statistics on abortions and unwed mothers. And they are increasing each year. There is no 100-percent safe method of birth control, short of sterilization—and even then accidents do happen.

9. There is an increased risk of cervical cancer among women who engage in sex with multiple partners.

That's a fact. I'm not making it up to scare you.

10. AIDS and other sexually transmitted diseases.

With most sexually transmitted diseases, such as gonorrhea, syphilis or herpes, you usually know within a few days or weeks whether you have contracted the disease because of obvious physical symptoms. AIDS, however, can stay dormant in your body for up to ten years before you have any symptoms. This means that for ten years a person with AIDS may be unknowingly infecting sexual partners with the AIDS virus. Now, that's frightening. Suddenly, staying a virgin—and marrying a virgin—may be a life-or-death matter.

Venereal disease is, in itself, extremely serious if not deadly. And add to this the emotional grief caused by the disease—that alone can ruin a life.

When I mentioned this fact to one of my friends, she told me about a young woman she knew in college who I'll call Cindy. Cindy was a pre-med major, looking forward to a bright future. She had high moral standards and had maintained them for twenty-three years. During her senior year she went through a couple of relationships, and ended up wondering if she would ever get married. Then Bill came along.

Bill was older, tall, dark, muscular and handsome—and he drove a racy sports car. Cindy felt truly loved for the first time in her life, but Bill was slow to make a commitment, even though they talked of marriage. On the night he begged her to have sex, she felt this might be the commitment she was looking for. Convinced he really loved her, Cindy said yes, even though all her moral training screamed no.

She gave him her virginity, and he gave her gonorrhea. The stigma of VD was almost more than Cindy could bear. When she confronted Bill, he claimed he had gotten the disease from her, which only added to her humiliation. Treatments were begun to heal the disease, but nothing could heal her guilt, not even counseling. For a year Bill would have nothing to do with her as he dated and conquered other women. This nearly destroyed Cindy, and her emotional agony resulted in her giving up her dream of medical school. Finally, when Bill came back to her, she said yes to marriage, in spite of the pain he had caused her.

They've been married for almost a year now, but most of Cindy's friends still question Bill's commitment. And Cindy will probably live with the consequences of her decision for life.

11. Research seems to indicate premarital sex isn't good for marriage.

Research findings indicate that those who have premarital sex tend to have less happy marriages, are more likely to have their marriages end in divorce, and are more likely to have extramarital affairs. Even though couples who had premarital sex seem to

achieve sexual satisfaction sooner after they are married, they are less satisfied overall with their marital
sex lives. That's sad, isn't it?

12. It destroys virginity.

Virginity is the one gift God has given to each
individual to give to his or her marriage partner. Having
premarital sex is like handing a million dollars to the
wrong person—and you can never get it back for the
right one.

13. It destroys reputations and respect.

It's almost impossible to keep premarital sex a
secret, no matter how hard you try. Eventually someone finds out, or one of the parties feels so guilty that
he or she confesses to a third party. What will this
knowledge do to your reputation? Do you have the right
to destroy another person's reputation? And what
about the respect you have for that person—and for
yourself?

Feelings of self-worth are important. If you do what
you know you shouldn't do, you demean your self-
respect, which is an important part of your total
feelings of self-worth. Are a few moments of sexual
pleasure worth the loss of your self-respect and someone else's?

14. It can destroy trust in a relationship.

Once premarital sex has occurred, there is a very
good chance that one or both partners may sometime
in the future question, "If this person had sex with me
outside the marriage relationship, would he or she do
it with someone else?" This leads to doubt, mistrust
and jealousy.

15. It destroys the value and meaning of the honeymoon.

This reason alone is enough to say no. Of course, it's difficult to understand the significance of a honeymoon when you've never experienced the excitement, the anticipation and the marvelous sense of fulfillment that is all intended to be a part of your wedding night. Trust me—there is nothing as special as a wedding night.

If you've had sex before marriage, the honeymoon becomes merely a vacation. That's crazy. You will be taking vacations for the rest of your life, but you'll only have one first honeymoon. More than anything else, your honeymoon is a sacred time to discover the love that God intended a man and a woman to experience. This should be your Eden experience—a little bit of heaven on earth.

16. Premarital sex tends to be habit-forming.

This is especially true when sex is experienced with a number of partners. If the sexual act no longer means a one-flesh commitment for life, then there is little to prevent a spouse from finding sexual partners outside the marriage relationship. When sex with various partners has been a habit, it's almost impossible for wives or husbands, no matter how good they may be in bed, to be able to continue to satisfy their spouses' increased appetite for novelty and change. It puts the spouse wanting a monogamous relationship in an almost impossible position. If you marry someone who has had multiple sexual partners, you may find their sexual appetite is difficult to satisfy.

17. Attitudes often change after a premarital sex experience.

Even though you and your boyfriend or girlfriend

think you are madly in love and your love will last a lifetime, premarital sex can do strange things to your feelings. Once you experience sex, you may no longer respect the other person. Like dominoes, all your loving feelings begin to tumble, and a reversion reaction sets in. Then, instead of having loving feelings toward your sexual partner, you feel resentful, angry and possibly used.

18. You never know whom you will marry.

It's not uncommon for a person to date someone for a year or so, and then end up marrying that person's sibling, cousin or best friend. Can you imagine the hurt and the guilt that would result if you had fooled around with one and ended up marrying the other?

19. It erodes a relationship with God.

Sex is God's gift to you to be used as He instructs. When His instructions are ignored and you misuse His gift, the guilt feelings may be so strong that if you are not willing to ask forgiveness and change your ways, you may think that the only way you can live without overwhelming guilt is to turn away from God. What a mistake.

How much better to follow King David's example in the Bible. He repented of his sin with Bathsheba, and he didn't turn bitter against God, even though there were terrible consequences to his sin. And in the end, God called David a man after His own heart. What an example to all those who have yielded to the temptation of sex.

Some young people have a negative picture of marriage. Perhaps they have grown up experiencing family violence and abuse. Others have listened to friends who have observed marriage as a "state of torment" instead of a "state of bliss." If this has been your experience, you may have developed the attitude that marriage isn't all that great, so why wait?

This is unfortunate. Marriage is truly a beautiful experience and the complete sexual experience is worth saving for your lifetime partner as a gift symbolizing a binding commitment. This is God's plan for your ultimate happiness.

Self-Stimulated Sexual Response

Sexual desire reaches its peak for men in the late teens and early twenties and for women in the twenties and early thirties. For many, this intense desire precedes the finding of a spouse and the yearning to settle down into a lifetime marriage relationship. If God created the sexual desire to peak so early, and if sex with someone outside of marriage is wrong, then what about self-stimulation? Masturbation is better than unmarried sex, isn't it?

There has been a lot of discussion about masturbation. Years ago it was taboo. It was believed masturbation caused all kinds of diseases, including blindness and insanity. Today scientists laugh at this. Even some Christian leaders have said that although masturbation isn't necessarily good, it's certainly a lot better than having intercourse with someone else. The problem, they say, is when you entertain lustful thoughts while engaging in self-stimulation, because Jesus specifically mentioned lust to be a sin (Matthew 5:27,28).

Others argue that there is no difference physiologically in the sexual response whether it is from genital penetration or hand-manipulation. Since there is still the excitement phase, the plateau, the climax, and finally the resolution phase, why is sexual intercourse in marriage so good, and masturbation so bad?

The answer is that sexual intercourse brings two people together in a closer relationship, while masturbation causes a person to draw away from relationships with others. There is a study on health habits that offers interesting insight. The study was done by two well-known epidemiologists, Nedra Belloc and Lester Breslow.[1] They found that if people kept seven health habits, they lived longer. The health habits were: getting adequate sleep, eating breakfast, not eating between meals, keeping a moderate weight, exercising, not smoking and drinking moderately or not at all.

When two social-epidemiologists, Lisa Berkman and Leonard Syme,[2] got involved, they asked, "If physical health habits are important for longevity, what about social health habits?" They used four questions from the health habits study that gave an indication of a person's social contacts: 1. Are you married? 2. Do you belong to a church? 3. Are you a member of any social clubs? 4. Do you have close friends and relatives? When they analyzed the data, they found that people who had these four things present in their lives lived longer, regardless of their physical health habits. In other words, we are social creatures and social contacts are important for health and longevity.

And what does this have to do with masturbation? Sexual intercourse is other-oriented—or should be! Masturbation, however, is merely for self-pleasure. Instead of building relationships, it may actually cause a person to become even more withdrawn. Those who habitually masturbate, sometimes multiple times per day, are often extremely isolated individuals.

One could apply the chicken and the egg argument to this and ask, "Is it the isolated individual who is drawn to masturbate, or does masturbation cause a person to become isolated?" Regardless, it does appear from research that those individuals who lack a social network and are more isolated don't live as long as others. The implication is that isolated people are less healthy. Could it be that masturbation, per se, may not cause illness, but that isolation does? It's something to consider.

Regardless of these suppositions, masturbation is using the sexual act to do exactly the opposite of what God intended sex to do. Instead of bringing two people closer together, masturbation has a tendency to alienate and isolate. It can also diminish the meaning of a one-flesh marriage commitment for life if lustful fantasies are entertained while a person stimulates him- or herself. Engaging in these fantasies can tempt individuals to fulfill their sexual appetites promiscuously.

Lust reduces a partner, even a fantasy partner, to merely an object. This results in further isolation (a person-to-object relationship) rather than true intimacy (a person-to-person relationship). And in far too many cases, the person who habitually masturbates is tempted to seek out pornographic material to heighten the sexual response.

Masturbation can, in some cases, affect an individual's adjustment to marital intercourse. When individuals get into the habit of masturbating, their attention is completely focused on their own arousal, so they soon learn how to bring about a quick and intense response. The objective of sexual intercourse, however, should be to pleasure your partner. Many who masturbate habitually are disappointed in their sexual response during intercourse. Because their minds are focused on their partner, their own response may not be as intense as it is when self-stimulated. To find satisfaction, too many of these individuals go back to masturbating rather than drawing close to their spouses and concentrating on learning how to pleasure them. The result? Isolation, alienation and, too often, divorce.

There is nothing wrong in touching your own body and being aware of what stimulates your sexual responsiveness. Good sexual adjustment in marriage is a result of feeling comfortable about your body, knowing what is pleasurable to you and communicating this to your partner. For many women, a sexual climax is not experienced in the early stages of marriage. In fact, some women go years without having a sexual climax simply because they don't know what stimulation their body needs in order to respond. There is nothing wrong with self-stimulation to learn this information, if the motive is to have a deeper enjoyment of the sexual relationship with a spouse.

But there is no need for extensive experimentation before marriage. In fact, if one chooses to participate in self-stimulation, there may develop an even greater desire for sexual activity, making it very difficult to control sexual urges. God didn't create you to be hot-wired, and then have no place to go. If you keep hot-wiring yourself by keeping your mind on sexual things, your body will crave release.

If you're having trouble in this area, take a look at your life. What music are you listening to? What pictures hang on your walls? What movies do you watch? What magazines do you look through? Are you eating a healthy diet? Are you getting good exercise? If you answered these questions the way I think you did, then no wonder you're having trouble!

If you keep your mind on serving others and becoming the kind of person God wants you to be, God can help you get through these years of sexual temptation so you can come to marriage with purity, and celebrate your union with God's symbol of a one-flesh, lifetime commitment.

Something to Think About . . .

Are you ready to commit your sexual desires to the Lord? Are you ready to trust Him and His plan for their fulfillment? If you've been struggling in this area, I encourage you to go before the Lord and honestly tell Him how you're feeling. Believe me, He won't be shocked at anything you say.

Notes

1. Nedra B. Belloc and Lester Breslow, "Relationship of Physical Health Status and Health Practices," *Preventive Medicine* (August 1972), pp. 409-421.
2. Lisa Berkman and Leonard Syme, "Social Networks Host Resistance and Mortality: A Nine Year Follow-Up Study of Alameda County Residents," *American Journal of Epidemiology*, Vol. 109 (February 1979), pp. 186-204.

• 10 •

Growing Toward Bonded Intimacy

We were never meant to be alone. God said it in the beginning, and it's still just as true. We need each other. In fact, we crave intimacy and fear isolation.

Many sexual relationships are entered into because of the mistaken idea that intimacy can only be achieved by having sex. But true intimacy is not physical—it's psychological. It can be psychological *and* physical, but never just physical. Because sex and intimacy are erroneously equated, too many lonely people jump into bed with strangers and end up dreadfully disillusioned. In their race to what they thought was intimacy, they miss the foundation stages of a relationship that make true intimacy possible.

Sex, apart from intimacy, is never psychologically satisfying. It may be a release for sexual tension and momentarily exhilarating, but the sex act alone will never fulfill a person's need for true intimacy. Intimacy is achieved when we bare our souls, not our bodies, to each other. It's the sharing of our innermost feelings that breaks the isolation barrier.

Sex is designed to be the crowning act of intimacy when a couple builds their relationship on the foundation of soul sharing and close fellowship, and then pledges their lifelong commitment to each other in marriage. If psychological intimacy has been achieved prior to marriage, then physical intimacy will cement the commitment. This combination of psychological and physical intimacy is what I call bonded intimacy. This is the ultimate! It's the mountaintop experience every young person dreams of having. It's the warm cozy feeling that happens when two people psychologically and physically become one. But bonded intimacy can only be experienced within the security of a marriage relationship.

And you can't rush it. Time is the bonding material. Far too many couples race through the friendship stage of their relationship and head off on their honeymoon without experiencing the psychological oneness that is the necessary foundation for bonded intimacy. They become married singles and wonder what went wrong. If you don't want this to happen to you, it is important you don't rush your love relationship. If you do rush and happen to miss a step or two, you will have to backtrack before you can experience the intimacy that God planned for you to find in marriage. So why not do it right the first time?

To help you on your journey toward bonded intimacy, I've created sixteen steps to go through and placed them into four relational stages: friendship dating, serious dating, courtship and marriage. Take the time to enjoy each step of your journey, won't you? The relationship you build will be worth your efforts.

Friendship Dating

The friendship stage of a relationship can be experienced with anyone, even though casual dating may occur during this time. The friendship stage is the foundation for bonded intimacy. If the steps in this stage are missed or rushed through, a couple will have to regress to this stage in order to achieve a complete sense of intimacy. The four steps within the friendship stage are as follows:

Step 1: Looking with interest at each other

There is usually something about a person's appearance, expression, words or demeanor that draws your attention to that person and makes you want to get acquainted. Every relationship starts out on this level.

Different individuals are attracted by different things. For one it might be the words of a person's prayer. For another it may be the sparkle in someone's eyes, or the way he walks, or she smiles. Something catches your attention and makes you desire a relationship.

If you don't immediately go over and introduce yourself, you begin planning how you can meet. You may talk to others about this person and take note of where he or she hangs out. You might phone or write to suggest a casual date so you can get acquainted. At this point the relationship quickly moves to Step 2.

Step 2: Getting acquainted

This time is characterized by conversation aimed at finding out about the other person: "Where did you go to school? How many brothers and sisters do you have? What classes are you taking? What career are you interested in?" At this level ideas and opinions are expressed, and you learn what makes a person unique. Discussions may range from current events to deep, theoretical issues. The end result, however, is the same—you get to know enough about the person to either walk away from the friendship or move forward.

It's during this level that you begin to discover similar interests, share ideas and assess whether the person's basic personality is pleasing. If you like what you're learning, you move on to the next step.

Step 3: Intimate talking and fellowship

Step 3 is probably the most important in the bonding process. You now begin to invest large amounts of time into this relationship, and you really get to know each other as you share your dreams, your feelings and what's on your heart. You develop a deep understanding about where you both are coming from and what makes each of you tick. You empathize with each other, hurting when he hurts, laughing when she laughs.

During this stage you begin to plan how you can spend more time together, and how you can let the other person know how special he or she is to you. Through words and actions, your message is, "I care."

You now become vulnerably honest. You bare your soul, so to speak, and you risk the possibility of being misunderstood and rejected. But it's the vulnerability that brings psychological closeness and satisfaction.

The intensity and time commitment required to continue this level of intimacy makes it impossible to have this type of friendship with more than just a few people. And such relationships may not be long-term. Usually, as the satisfaction level of one "psychologically intimate" relationship wanes, another is started, until a person finds a relationship with someone of the opposite sex that is so satisfying it can move satisfactorily into the dating stage, which is the next important stage in bonded intimacy. But before we discuss the dating stage there is one more step within the friendship stage.

Step 4: Meaningful touching

For some, touch comes easy. I've watched my

daughter, for example, cross the college campus and spontaneously hug various people she meets. It's her way of saying, "hello," and it has little to do with intimacy. Other individuals find it almost impossible to touch others, regardless of how close the friendship. Some have been raised in families or cultures where physical contact is taboo. Others have been hurt so deeply that they are afraid to reach out to others for fear that they will be rejected.

Because touch is an essential step in achieving intimacy, and because so many people have felt inhibited in this area, touch-oriented encounter groups have gained popularity. Many professionals have reasoned that if people could become vulnerable to touch, they could experience intimacy. The problem is that touch alone, without intimate talking and fellowship, doesn't bring intimacy. Touch—that spontaneous hug or the reaching out for another person's hand—is a natural outgrowth of close, intimate sharing and fellowship.

During Steps 3 and 4 the desire for a more permanent relationship, which includes more physical contact, begins to build. And if it progresses satisfactorily, the relationship will now move to the dating stage.

Serious Dating

During this stage, friendship or casual dating (where the couple is becoming acquainted with each other) takes on a more serious nature. There is now a desire to date on a steady basis and to become more physically involved. And with physical involvement comes bonding—a psychological attachment to each other brought about through touch. If the physical relationship advances without the psychological intimacy of friendship, it is possible to become physically bonded to another person regardless of your personalities, interests or cultural differences. As long as physical intimacy is experienced, the couple "feels" bonded. The relationship seems "right." But something is missing.

Psychological intimacy and psychological attachment are not the same. Psychological intimacy is a feeling of oneness. Psychological attachment, caused by physical bonding, leads to dependency, not intimacy. The problem with attachment without intimacy is that you can't go through life constantly holding on to each other. Sooner or later you'll discover that the only thing you have in common is your physical attraction. Unless a couple goes back to Step 3 and begins to build a psychologically intimate friendship, the dependency relationship eventually crumbles.

Physical intimacy will come—don't rush it. And it will grow more meaningful and fulfilling, but only when it is built on psychological intimacy and not attachment. So don't advance through these next stages unless your friendship has been well established.

Step 5: Desiring physical touch

The desire to hold hands, kiss and embrace may have been present from the moment of attraction, but now this desire is no longer inhibited. And the result is that the steps toward more physical involvement are usually moved through rather quickly.

Step 6: Side-by-side hand holding symbolizing togetherness

Now the couple has a desire to let the world know about their special friendship. They want to be seen as a couple and they hold hands in public to symbolize their relationship.

Step 7: Touching that draws together

When the arm is placed around the shoulder or the waist, it symbolizes the couple being drawn together in a special way. Usually an arm around the shoulder comes first. Moving the hand down the body to waist-level symbolizes a more intimate relationship.

Step 8: Friendship kissing

Although a friendship kiss may have been placed on the hand, cheek or lips of a friend during the friendship stage, kissing now becomes more frequent and more intense. Once kissing becomes an expected part of a relationship, a couple enters a danger zone. Why? Because mouth-to-mouth kissing is sexually arousing and can quickly lead to other touching behavior that prepares the body for intercourse.

There is nothing wrong with a simple goodnight kiss, but when a couple engages in French kissing, the body becomes excited and there is a desire for sexual release. This desire can move a dating relationship toward marriage before the couple is psychologically prepared for a lifelong commitment.

Courtship

Courtship is the transition stage between dating and marriage. You have made the decision that the person you're dating is a suitable marriage partner. With this realization, the desire for physical intimacy is increased.

Step 9: Arousal kissing

Arousal kissing is like an explosive bombshell in a dating relationship. Once this bombshell goes off, it is very hard, if not impossible, to backtrack physically. When awakened to the intense feelings of passion, your body desires more. That's the way God designed a man and a woman. Without control in this area, a relationship can quickly—sometimes too quickly—be swept through the other courtship steps.

Step 10: Pleasuring each other with touch to non-sexual areas

Here's where rubbing someone's back, gently stroking the arms, legs or head, and tracing the lips or nose with your fingers becomes a natural part of the relationship. You feel comfortable touching each other. This type of touching is not always initiated with the motive to sexually arouse the other. It is merely an expression of deep desire and caring. It is satisfying just to know that someone has accepted you so completely that touch can be experienced without hesitation. Being comfortable with touch is an important step toward bonded intimacy. The next steps represent more passionate and intimate touching experiences.

Step 11: Extended embracing

Words of love and endearment usually accompany extended holding, kissing and stroking (sometimes called petting). Now you feel comfortable just being in someone else's arms, and you yearn to be held for long periods of time. At last you feel like you belong to someone.

Step 12: Talking about sexual expectations within marriage

Words exchanged during courtship can hurl a relationship forward more quickly than a couple may realize. Talking about sexually explicit acts, making comments about your own or your partner's sexual arousal, and discussing what turns you on is private talk. It's like psychologically undressing in front of someone. *And it has a bonding effect.*

This, of course, is a natural part of a courtship relationship. These things should be shared before marriage, but sharing them too soon may lead to an unspoken commitment to each other before psychological intimacy is experienced. Once certain things have been said, you will never again be truly private. Through words, you have given up a part of yourself that you can never get back.

Sexually explicit talk should be reserved for the last few months before marriage, since the next step toward bonded intimacy is to experience physically what you have expressed in words.

Marriage

Sexual stimulation beyond arousal kissing and stroking of non-sexual body parts should be reserved for marriage. If you limit your physical involvement in this way, the next four steps toward bonded intimacy will be celebrated on your wedding night and, hopefully, as often as possible throughout the years of your marriage. The result will be the blending of two separate individuals to form an intimate relationship that is bonded by sex—and continues to be bonded by sex.

Enjoy the first twelve steps of the bonding process to the fullest during the months of your courtship, and leave the last four to celebrate within the context of a committed lifetime love relationship. If you do, you will experience the intimacy that God designed you to have within marriage. If you don't, the chances are great that you'll experience sex without intimacy and be deeply disappointed.

Because this book isn't a marriage manual, the

last four steps toward bonded intimacy are only listed. These will occur in rather rapid succession as you discover each other within the bonds of marriage.

Step 13: Arousal kissing plus touching clothed body parts, including breasts, buttocks and genitals

Step 14: Foreplay

Step 15: Genital stimulation

Step 16: Intercourse

Once Bonded, Not Always Bonded

Many people feel that like epoxy glue, once you're bonded, you're always bonded. But that is not so. Human relationships need regular rebonding experiences to maintain intimacy—even within marriage. Each day should be started with Step 1 of the bonded intimacy process as you notice things about the other which you find attractive—things that make you want to renew your relationship. You and your partner are constantly changing. Each day you are a slightly different person than you were the day before. That's why you need to spend time getting acquainted with each other as you did in Step 2, sharing your ideas and opinions. If you don't, it may not be long before you're living with a stranger.

The problem with most marriages, and why very few couples experience the intimacy they thought they would find within marriage, is that they skip Step 3 (the sharing of feelings and fellowship) and move right on to Step 4 (a friendship hug or meaningful touch). They then advance quickly through arousal kissing and the rest of the sixteen steps, thinking that the sexual experience is all they need to keep their marriage intact. There is no shortcut, however, to continued intimacy. Without investing the time it takes to bare your soul daily to one another, you may have fleeting moments of oneness, but true intimacy—bonded intimacy—will never be yours.

Bonding and Breakup

Bonds can be broken. A breakup can occur anywhere along this process of growth toward bonded intimacy. The important thing to remember is that just as it takes time to become bonded, it also takes time to become unbonded. The further along in the process you are when a breakup occurs, the more painful the breakup will be and the longer it will take to become free from the bonds you have established.

I have known men and women who intellectually were convinced that marriage to a certain person would spell disaster, yet they allowed themselves to move so far up the steps to bonded intimacy that breaking up was almost impossible. Weeks, months, and sometimes years later, they still dreamed about the person and suffered feelings of loss and regret.

It is a mistake to believe that your feelings of loss will go away if you can just become intimately involved in another relationship. It is possible to be double-bonded. You can be in love with two people at the same time. This is the most agonizing relational condition you could ever find yourself in, because you doom yourself to disappointment and your loved ones to frustration and bitterness.

Do yourself a favor: Bury the old before getting seriously involved with the new. Sometimes that means destroying or putting away items that carry memories of that other person. There may be certain people whom you hung around with that bring back old memories.

You may need to work on making new friendships so the ties to the old can be lengthened. Sometimes you'll need a complete change in environment because everything you see reminds you of your old love.

Kyla was double-bonded. She intellectually knew that Mark, her old high school boyfriend whom she had dated for five years, would not treat her with the respect she wanted from a husband. She met another man who had all the qualities she was looking for and she loved him, but she was constantly haunted by old memories. Everywhere she turned she was reminded of Mark.

Depression followed. She thought she was going crazy. A good physical examination revealed some nutritional imbalances in her system which were corrected. And through the help of a counselor she decided to attend a college across the country to distance herself from anything that would remind her of her old love. Good health, time and distance healed the double-bonding.

If you think you need help giving up a past relationship, go to a trained counselor. Talking things through with a professional will help you sort out your feelings, allow you to put away the past and give you the freedom to move into the future.

The Bonding Power of First Love

May individuals who have broken up after experiencing the intense closeness of the bonding experience find themselves questioning love the second time around. Though they have an intimate friendship relationship, want more physically and feel this person is the ideal mate, for some reason the intense feelings of the first-love experience are just not there. They question, "Is this true love?"

If you find yourself asking this question, remember that the intensity of feeling you experienced the first time around is not a true barometer to measure the type of love that will make it through a lifetime. You are a different person now. Older. You see things more maturely. The strength of bonded intimacy is not the fickleness of feeling; it is much deeper, more meaningful and more satisfying. If the relationship is psychologically intimate, feelings will follow.

Bonding does not happen by suddenly falling in love. Bonding is a process—a series of steps that two people go through as they become more psychologically and physically involved with each other. The end result is a growing sense of intimacy that in marriage has the potential of becoming bonded intimacy—the mountaintop experience every couple dreams of but very few take the time to sustain.

Make bonded intimacy your goal—and enjoy each step of your journey along the way.

❤ ❤ ❤

Something to Think About . . .

Evaluate your present relationship (or a previous one if you're not currently involved with someone). Have you skipped any of the steps to bonded intimacy? What can you do to backtrack and work on that area of your relationship? List three things you can do in the next few months to specifically meet the need of the step (or steps) you have missed.

❤ 11 ❤

Courtship
Communication

"Now that it's all over," said one old-timer to another, "which do you think was worse, Watergate or the Contra Affair?"

"Well," replied his friend, "I haven't thought about water gates and irrigation for so long, I don't really have an opinion on that. But I am definitely against affairs."

We laugh at the obvious misunderstanding. But the sad fact is that a lack of communication is no laughing matter, especially when it comes to marriage.

I once asked a pastor, who spent the majority of his time counseling couples in conflict, what he considered to be the three most important things couples could do to keep their marriages vibrant and alive. He responded, "Number 1: Talk. Number 2: Talk. And Number 3: Talk!" Marital success depends on keeping the channels of communication open.

It doesn't take long for a lack of communication to destroy a marriage. That's why it's important to learn the principles of good communication during your courtship. *Now* is the time to listen for the feelings behind the words, tune into body language and learn how to say what's on your mind so it sounds to the other person "like apples of gold in settings of silver"

(Proverbs 25:11), and not like "continual dripping on a very rainy day" (Proverbs 27:15). (You'll have to look up those texts to get the full significance!)

Most of us talk without thinking. We say exactly what's on our minds, and that's what gets us into trouble. But with a little thought and some training, you can smooth out the rough edges of what you say, so you can get your message across without causing hard feelings or becoming frustrated.

There's no better time to learn these skills than now, during the dating and courtship period of your life. What follows are some of the most important principles of effective communication. If you faithfully follow these guidelines, hopefully by the time you say, "I do," these patterns will have become habitual, and the potential for conflict between the two of you will be significantly reduced.

Principle 1: Never say anything you wouldn't want someone to say to you.

It may need to be said, but think first. How would you want this message delivered to you? Cushion your words in the kindest language possible. Applying the Golden Rule, to treat others as you want to be treated, will save you much grief—and a lot of apologies.

Principle 2: Share your feelings before you are forced to act them out.

Some think that rather than risk an argument, a person should bury negative emotions and try to forget them. But buried feelings don't die. Instead, they grow in the dark places of your heart until they end up causing either ulcers or explosions—neither of which is very good for your health or your relationship.

Here's what to do: Learn to recognize a negative feeling when it first appears and do something immediately to get rid of it while it's still small and manageable. If you do, you won't have to act it out later when it's big and ugly and can no longer be contained. When you lose control and act out negative feelings, such as anger or jealousy, it's quite likely that you will do or say something that will end up hurting someone. And the problem only gets worse, not better.

Let's say my husband forgets to kiss me when he leaves for work. I feel hurt, but I don't do anything about that negative feeling. Instead, I harbor it in my heart and allow it to grow. Soon I'm not only feeling hurt, but also disappointed and upset about his lack of attention. By lunchtime I'm angry and decide that it's time he takes some responsibility for this relationship. But instead of calling him, I sit by the phone and wait for him to call me. Of course, you can guess what happens—he doesn't call. Now I'm furious at him and my negative feeling leads to revengeful behavior. I decide to teach him a lesson by spending his entire paycheck on myself.

My small, almost insignificant hurt feeling has now turned into a hurtful action that will probably end up making my husband angry. And that's when the sparks begin to fly.

There is a better way to deal with negative feelings. Let's go back and put a different ending to the story. When my husband forgets to kiss me, let's say I recognize immediately that I'm feeling hurt. This time I choose to share that small feeling before it has a chance to grow. I must act quickly, so I run after him as he backs the car out of the driveway, calling, "Honey, you forgot to kiss me and I'm feeling hurt."

What man in his right mind would continue down the driveway? Instead, he'll probably stop and give me a better than average kiss, and my negative feeling will go away.

The key to controlling negative feelings, so they don't damage a relationship, is to immediately do something to get rid of them before they get out of hand.

Principle 3: Listen to the other person's feelings.

Feelings can be expressed in words as well as body language, so we must learn to pay attention to both. It has been estimated that only 10 percent of what we actually communicate comes from our words, while 25 percent is from the tone of our voice and 65 percent comes from non-verbal body language. Because non-verbal communication is so important, we must learn to listen to more than words.

Another time to be sure to look beyond the words is when we are confronted with something that sounds a little critical. Our tendency is to get so wrapped up in trying to defend ourselves that we don't listen carefully to what is being said.

However, if you perceive a negative emotion in what's being said, allow the person to talk about it. Look interested and say something like, "You feel angry about what I just did. I can tell by the way you looked at me." Then be quiet and give the other person a chance to voice what's on his or her heart.

If any advice could top the counsel to talk, talk, talk, it would be to listen, listen, listen. If you follow these words of wisdom when you or your partner are experiencing negative emotions, you'll find these feelings will be defused and will probably go away. So be willing to talk *and* to listen!

Principle 4: Avoid door-slammers that cut off communication.

A "door-slammer" is what is usually said right before someone screams, "Why can't you understand me!" These are words or phrases that inhibit conversation rather than encourage it. Door-slammers hurt people's feelings and make them want to retreat rather than stick around and listen to more. Here are a few of the most popular door-slammers.

Commanding: "I thought I told you to return those books to the library."

Threatening: "If you can't remember to return the books on time, you're just going to have to pay the fine."

Moralizing: "If you would just do what you were supposed to do, life would be much more pleasant."

Giving advice: "Next time write down what you are supposed to do so you won't forget."

Arguing: "Don't try to give me some lame excuse. The simple fact is that you forgot."

Criticizing: "You're always forgetting to do what you are supposed to do. Why can't you use your head for what it's meant to be used for?"

Ridiculing: "If you tied a string around your finger, you'd probably forget what it was there for."

Analyzing: "One of the reasons you are so forgetful is probably because you have so much on your mind and don't listen to me when I'm trying to tell you something."

Questioning: "You forgot to return the books! Why did you do that?"

Withdrawing: "I don't want to hear about it. It's your problem, not mine."

Sympathizing: "Oh, you poor baby. You must feel terrible about forgetting those books."

Patronizing: "You're such a perfect person. You're *always* so reliable and trustworthy. That's why I'm surprised you forgot."

Just think about how you'd feel if these things were said to you. Would it make you want to continue a conversation? I doubt it. Chances are, after too many of these comments, you'd throw up your hands in frustration, run to your room and slam the door!

Principle 5: Use door-openers for better understanding.

Instead of the door-slammer approach, why don't you try these five door-opener techniques? These nice warm fuzzy messages encourage continued sharing.

The first door-opener is *body language*. Show that you are listening by looking at the other person's eyes, leaning forward and using a facial expression of interest.

Second, use *acknowledgments* such as, "Yes," "Oh," "That's interesting," "Hmmm," and other audible comments to show you are interested and listening.

Third, *silence*. Yes, silence can be positive, especially when used with interested body language and a few acknowledgments that show you care. Silence can give the space a person needs to think about what to say next. When you are silent and using positive body language, you are non-verbally saying, "I want to hear what is happening to you, and I'm going to be quiet long enough to hear it." Or, "I accept your feelings, whatever they are. I am not here to change you." Or, "I trust you to decide what you want to say to me. You are in charge of those decisions right now."

Silence is only effective when your body language says, "I'm listening." When silence is used too often or for too long of a time, it is counter-productive.

Fourth, offer *invitations* for the person to say more, like: "Would it help to talk about it?" "It is hard to talk about some things." "Tell me in your own way." "How is it going for you?" "That's interesting." Or, "Anything else?"

Fifth, *reflecting*, or restating what the person has said in slightly different words, is a great way to open the door to more conversation. Reflection lets the other person know you are listening and checks your understanding of what he or she means. For example, if someone spouts, "I felt like hauling off and hitting that guy after what he said to me," a reflection to that comment might be, "It hurt you when he spoke so harshly," or "You weren't prepared for his tirade," or "It's no fun to be verbally abused." Do you get the idea? A reflection is a non-judgmental statement that gives the other person permission to continue talking.

Principle 6: Never walk away from an argument and pout.

There is nothing that makes a person feel more rejected than to have a loved one go silent, especially when you're in the middle of a conflict that desperately needs to be resolved.

Giving someone the silent treatment—or pouting—is childish. Everyone gets their feelings hurt occasionally, but the mature thing to do is to face the problem and solve it. The worst thing you can do is retreat. Instead of leading to reconciliation, the silent treatment too often results in isolation. It doesn't take most married couples long to discover that there is nothing quite as big as a bed with two pouting people in it! Believe it or not, some strong-willed couples have lived with "polite" silence for years, each so angry at the other that they would rather starve to death than break down and say, "Please, pass the potatoes."

Of course, you don't want this to happen to your relationship. But the chances are quite high that there will be times ahead when you will feel so frustrated with each other that you'll have to resist the natural urge to pout or walk away in silence.

There is a way to deal with those situations. Put the reason for your "walking away" behavior into written words. Next time you're ready to give the silent treatment, try saying, "You are not listening to me and I feel like clamming up or walking away and slamming the door. When I talk with you, I sometimes feel I don't get a fair chance to express myself. It's important to me that you understand where I'm coming from. I don't want to talk about it anymore right now because I'm having trouble communicating my feelings. Instead, I'd like to take a half hour or so to write down how I'm feeling. Then I'd like you to read it and we can discuss it. But promise me you won't be defensive or critical. Just listen to what I have to say and let's try to solve this problem. If we still have trouble communicating, I'd like you to write your response to me."

Writing down an argument may seem like a waste of time, but it does a number of very important things. First, when you are forced to write down how you feel, you begin to clarify your thinking and often the result is that your written words will make more sense than what you say "off the top of your head."

Second, writing your responses gives both of you time to think about what the other has said without being influenced by a tone of voice or body language. You can read and reread the message. Many times this reflection period allows tense hostile feelings to mellow, and your responses to each other are more civil and much more conducive to solving the problem.

To cushion your written response and make it as palatable as possible, here are a few helpful techniques. Start your written message with a prayer for your partner, and then add a sincere compliment. This cushions the tough stuff which is the heart of your message. To soften your close you might want to add another prayer or an honest word of appreciation.

You'll be surprised how effective this method is for solving conflicts. But you'll never really know until you try.

Principle 7: Confront each other with "I-messages," not "You-messages."

An "I-message" allows you to take the responsibility for what has happened. A "You-message" blames the other person. Note the difference: "_I_ get angry when _I_ find newspapers and dirty clothes all over the place," versus, "_You_ are so messy. Why can't _you_ put the newspapers where they belong and toss _your_ dirty clothes in the hamper?"

It's not easy to keep the _you_ out of a message when you are convinced that if the other person would just shape up, everything would be fine. But the safest way to confront someone with something you don't like is to keep the _you_ completely out of the message. This takes practice. To get you started, change the following "You-messages" into statements that avoid the _you_ completely. If you get stumped, you'll find possible answers at the end of the chapter. But don't peak at my answers until you've tried to come up with your own.

1. "I don't like it when you use my things without asking."

2. "I am tired of listening to you gripe about my parents."

3. "I feel jealous when you spend so much time with other people."

Principle 8: Don't try to solve problems when you're angry.

Once you have listened to each other's feelings, and those feelings have been defused or diminished, you can successfully solve a problem, *but not before*. When most couples get angry with each other they make the mistake of trying to solve the problem immediately. The result is usually a shouting match which ends up with both opponents hurling verbal weapons at each other. That's no way to solve a problem. Verbal conflict only causes emotional wounds, and may even lead to physical abuse.

When you both are eager for a resolution to your conflict but you are upset, you should carefully and prayerfully go through the following problem-solving steps.

First, clarify the problem. What is it that you disagree about? Be as specific as possible. There may be a number of issues involved, but it's best to deal with one at a time.

Second, begin brainstorming about possible solutions. Don't try to evaluate your ideas during this stage or you may reject a crazy idea that could turn out to be a creative solution. Accept every suggestion, no matter how off the wall it may seem. When you have exhausted all the possibilities, you can move on to the next step.

Third, evaluate your brainstorming ideas, discarding those that are unacceptable to either of you. As you attempt to find a solution, look for ways to compromise by combining two possible solutions or making slight changes in one idea so it becomes acceptable to both of you. The key to success at this point is your willingness to find a solution, which means being ready to compromise.

Fourth, choose the best solution and determine when it will be put into effect. If you can, pick a specific date.

Fifth, indicate in some way that you both accept

this solution. Kiss, bring out the cherry cheese cake and celebrate, or sign on the dotted line!

Sixth, continue to evaluate the situation to make sure the solution is working. If it isn't working, you've got to go back to the bargaining table and begin brainstorming again.

There is no problem so difficult that two people *willing to compromise* can't solve. The key is that both people in a relationship must be willing to compromise. Solutions are never acceptable when one person consistently must give in to the other in order for problems to be "solved."

Principle 9: Agree on some basic rules for communicating feelings.

Here are some rules you might want to establish early in your relationship. They'll help you keep your discussions about feelings "fair" so you can avoid conflict during those vulnerable moments.

Rule 1: Feelings are neither good nor bad, they just are. If you feel them, regardless of whether they are reasonable or not, *they are real* and must be listened to and healed with understanding.

Rule 2: Each person owns his or her own feelings. In other words, you choose whether to let something somebody else says or does bother you. An expression of a negative feeling should not be interpreted as personal criticism. Here's an example. When your boyfriend says, "I feel angry when you're not on time," you could take it to mean, "It's all your fault. If you were on time, I wouldn't be angry." This will probably cause you to become defensive, and an argument usually results.

How much better if you both agree that you will be responsible for your own reactions. A person doesn't make you angry—you choose to allow a certain situation to make you angry. When you own your own feelings, you're able to discuss these feelings without the fear that you will hurt the other person's ego or cause them to become defensive. Talking about emotions helps to defuse them.

Don't resent it when someone mentions a negative feeling. Instead, use the door-opener techniques to encourage the person with the feeling to talk about it. Maybe you could respond, "It embarrasses you when I make you late for an appointment." When the emotion has been defused, you can add, "How should we solve the problem?"

Rule 3: Don't bring up controversial topics unless you both have the time and energy to finish the conversation. Sometimes you may need to put hot topics on the back burner until you both are ready to deal with them. But be up front and say, "I want to discuss the way I feel when we go to parties together, but now is not a good time. When do you think you would have time to sit down and spend some time resolving this issue?" Or you might simply say, "I need to talk with you about a few things. It's not urgent, but I think it might take a while. When is a good time for you?"

Rule 4: If something is bothering you, don't bury it. Promise each other you will not walk away from an issue that needs to be talked about and solved. If you can't do it immediately, make an appointment.

Rule 5: If either one of you feels unsatisfied with the way you're communicating, agree that you will go to a counselor. You may not feel the need for a counselor, but if the other person does, that is reason enough to go and seek help. If followed, this rule would prevent many divorces.

Principle 10: Avoid habits of speech that annoy others.

Annoying habits of speech get in the way of effective communication. Here are a dozen of the most offensive:

1. Not looking at the other person when you are talking to them

   Eye-to-eye contact is important.

2. Using big impressive words

   Gargantuan instead of *huge,* for example.

3. Repeating yourself

   Say something once and move on—don't say it over and over to try to get your point across.

4. Excessive agreement

   Always agreeing, no matter what someone else says, gets obnoxious.

5. Excessive disagreement

   It's also obnoxious when someone constantly takes the antagonist position.

6. Talking too much

   No one likes to be around someone who has to comment about everything. It's especially offensive when the person is always talking about himself.

7. Quibbling over minutia

   Some things are so insignificant that it's not worth arguing about. What's annoying is when someone is constantly picking an argument over something so insignificant that it really doesn't matter.

8. Under-responsiveness

Have you ever tried to have a conversation with someone who hardly ever responds?

"Wasn't it a super game?"

"It was okay."

"What did you think about that ninth inning double that tied the score?"

"Okay."

"And that pitcher was something else!"

"Ya."

Do you get the idea? No one wants to get stuck on a date with an under-responder, much less marry one!

9. Making over-generalizations

"She's always talking." "He never dresses right." "You always get the last word." Seldom is something "always" or "never." Be specific. If you like something that someone does, say, "Hey, that was a neat piano solo," rather than, "You always play perfectly." And, "You wore that yellow tie last week," is more acceptable than, "You always wear the same thing."

10. Making illogical comments

It's really aggravating when you are deep in a conversation and someone says something that's way out in left field—completely irrelevant. Keep on the subject and your contribution to a conversation will be a lot more meaningful.

11. Making assumptions without adequate information

Let's say you've said something like, "The party wasn't what I expected." It's just a simple statement of fact. The last thing you need is somebody making an assumption like, "Well, I know why you didn't enjoy it.

Bonnie wasn't there. You two just can't get along without each other."

12. Put-downs and pessimism

No one likes an habitual pessimist who can't find anything good to say about anybody or anything. It's unsafe to be around someone who is always critical because chances are you'll be criticized next. Lift people up, don't put them down, and you'll be a much more desirable conversationalist.

What Is Good Communication?

Good communication is a dialogue, not a monologue. Listen to what Elizabeth O'Connor, in her book *Cry Pain, Cry Hope*, has to say about this:

> Dialogue is more than your giving me space to say my words, and my giving you space to say yours. It involves our listening. We are all different. We cannot have dialogue unless we honor the differences. How can I build a bridge across the gulf between me and you unless I am aware of the gulf? How can I communicate with you unless I see how things look from your side?

> Dialogue demands that I leave the place where I dwell—the landscape of feelings and thoughts that are important to me—in order to dwell for a time with your thoughts, feelings, perceptions, fears, hopes. I must deny myself—forsake the familiar, give up my life—in order to experience your life.

> The purpose of dialogue is never to persuade another person to accept our opinions, or values, or view of the world; rather it is to create understanding—a climate where communion takes place. He who has lost himself finds himself. The deepest craving of every heart is to be laid bare, to be known, to be understood . . .

But how many of us can take time to understand, or even time to make ourselves understood?
There is always some place to go, or something to do,
secrets to protect.

And if we do not take time to understand each
other, how can we take time to understand God?[1]

It's something to think about, isn't it?

Communication is what keeps a relationship alive.
Don't let a day slip by without it. In fact, you would be
wise to plan "talk-time" into your schedule. Maybe you
would enjoy taking a long walk together each evening,
or turning off the television while you eat so you can
talk without interruption. This planned communication time will become even more important after
marriage where you'll find there is the tendency to get
wrapped up in your own personal schedule or dis-
tracted by children.

Start practicing the principles of good communication during your courtship. Don't get married without
it.

❤   ❤   ❤

Something to Think About . . .

Think of the communication you have not only with the
person you're dating, but also with your friends, your
family and your co-workers. When does communication break down? What can you do to improve
communication between you and those you come in
contact with? Pick one of the principles mentioned in
this chapter and consciously work at incorporating it
into your life.

Notes

1. Elizabeth O'Connor, *Cry Pain, Cry Hope* (Waco, TX: Word, Inc., 1987), pp. 39-40.

Answers to "You-Messages"/"I-Messages"

1. "I don't like it when my things get used without my permission."

2. "I am tired of hearing my parents criticized." Or, "It makes me angry when my parents are criticized."

3. "I feel jealous when other people seem to get more of your attention than I get."

♥ 12 ♥

Discovering the Difference Between Romantic Illusions and True Love

It beckoned you from your earliest moments of memory. It captured you through the excitement of Barbie doll play. Its mystique stimulated your imagination and your wildest fantasies. You experienced it in brief encounters. You read about it in novels. You were reminded of it on every billboard. Its music filled your world. It fluttered your heart, made you lose your senses, and became the controlling desire of your life.

Beware of the powerful force of romantic love. It is merely an illusion that fades all too quickly. It's only true love that has the beautiful blend of passion and accountability, spontaneity and design, tenderness and strength, innocence and reason. It's the kind of love that can last a lifetime.

Romantic love or infatuation is short-term and has only the passion. It's a totally absorbing type of love, binding two people in a whirlwind of bliss that makes them oblivious to reason and reality. Romantic love is blind!

Romantic love can grow into lifetime love if a couple has no hidden pathology from their pasts, and if their personalities are compatible, their interests are similar and their commitment to each other is based on more than feelings. But you can never assume that this intense short-term love will simmer into a lifelong love affair.

Marriage should never take place during the passionate stage of a romance. It all seems so wonderful, so how can you tell what type of love you are experiencing? You'll find your answer by carefully, and as rationally as possible, considering the answers to the following questions. It might also be helpful to ask your parents or close friends how they see your relationship.

1. Has your lover swept you off your feet in a whirlwind romance that has taken your breath away and left you weak-kneed?

If yes, be careful. True love doesn't happen suddenly. Regardless of what you may have heard, no one really falls in love at first sight. You may be attracted to each other and feel an immediate emotional high. You may have sensed, from the moment your eyes met, that you were right for each other. You may feel in love.

But true love, love that will last a lifetime, takes time to develop. Don't rush a good thing. Savor every day of love as a gift from God. And if it is meant to be, it will pass the test of time.

2. Are you more in love when you are together than when you are by yourself? Or are you in love with the writer of love letters and find yourself confused when you are together?

Love does not fluctuate according to the presence or absence of the one you love. If you love a person more when you are together, chances are that your judgment is being influenced by the charm and excitement of his or her presence. When your loved one is not around to dazzle you, some doubts emerge.

Or the opposite can be true. You may be in love with an image that is portrayed through beautifully written words. But when you are together, the reality of looks, actions and speech makes you question your feelings. It is possible to fall in love by merely exchanging love letters. Don't let your feelings be swayed by the poetic beauty of words. And be careful not to let your own written words cause you to commit yourself to a relationship with someone you really haven't spent that much time with.

Love is stable, not up and down depending on whether you are together or not. Unstable love is superficial. It can grow into true love, but it takes time.

3. Would you be jealous and upset if someone else made a serious play for your loved one?

Jealousy is not a sign of true love. One of the greatest mistakes young people make is to believe that the more violent the jealousy, the stronger the love. A fleeting jealous thought may occur in certain situations when two people who care deeply for each other have not yet made a lasting commitment. But prolonged or irrational feelings of jealousy signify possessiveness, not love.

People who suffer acutely from jealousy often have an underlying sense of insecurity which leads to an overwhelming need to be loved and to control the lover. As a result, a person can be extremely jealous even though he or she may not be in love at all. Love, says 1 Corinthians 13:7, "bears all things, believes all things, hopes all things, endures all things."

Jealousy in marriage can kill the love two people once experienced. Instead of setting the other person free to become everything God wants that person to become, jealousy constrains the other. And this lack of trust, this irrational jealousy, can easily turn feelings of affection into feelings of hostility. Don't get involved with someone who is irrationally jealous before marriage. The wedding ceremony seldom makes much difference.

4. Do both of you have a substantial number of complaints in common about home, parents, school and other things in your lives?

Most people agree that there cannot be real love unless two persons share common interests. But being companions in misery is not the same as being in love. Marriage partners should be able to share miseries and heartaches, but such sharing is not in itself love. All too frequently couples mix up the two and enter into marriage simply because each has discovered a fellow sufferer with whom to unite against an unfriendly world.

Too often marriage becomes an escape from some unfortunate situation and too late the couple wakes up to the realization that they have jumped into an equally unfortunate situation. An unhappy home life can trick you into thinking you're in love.

Reesie is a good example of this. She was constantly battling her parents. When Phil came along she saw him as her knight in shining armor who was going to rescue her from her problems. She thought she was in love, but she wasn't. She just wanted a legitimate way to escape the control of her parents.

5. Has your personality, behavior or attitudes changed during this courtship?

You should be happier and healthier if you are in love. True love makes you want to be and do your very best. It should bring your most positive traits to the surface. Your container of love should be so full that it overflows to others.

Sometimes it is difficult to assess yourself, so ask your friends, teachers or parents. Are you more fun to be around? Are you more responsible? Are you more thoughtful?

If your positive behavior has deteriorated, something is wrong. Are you neglecting others in an effort to focus on the one for whom you have fallen? This is a sign of infatuation. Before announcing your engagement, give yourself time to settle into a love relationship that is so full it spills over to other relationships. If it's really love, your friends and family will affirm to you that you are a better and happier person now than before.

6. Is your relationship with your parents strained?

A true love relationship should enhance all relationships, including your relationship with your parents. When you begin to invest your life in the life of your lover, there is a natural drawing away from Mom and Dad. You no longer spend as much time with them as you might have in the past. And you now have someone else to confide in, so your need for intimate communication with your parents is less. But this doesn't have to cause a strained relationship. True love should not cause hard feelings or rejection. Instead, the love you are feeling for each other should cause you to treat your parents with more kindness, thankfulness and respect.

7. When you aren't with your lover, do you find yourself sighing and daydreaming?

If so, this is another indication of infatuation. Genuine love is centered in the other person, with your whole behavior directed toward his or her welfare and happiness. Thus, a couple in love can study and work comfortably, knowing they are contributing to each other's happiness. Romantic love, in contrast, is self-centered. The smitten one becomes absorbed in his or her own misery at being separated from the adored one. This is a sign of being in love with love, and not with a human being.

8. *Are you always anxious or on guard to make sure you are at your best when you are together? Are you conscious of what you say and how you look or act?*

Love doesn't make lovers feel ill at ease. When you are still trying to impress the other person, *you* are the dominant concern in the relationship, not the other person. Real love is beyond that. When you experience true unconditional love, when you know that you are loved for who you are, you feel comfortable and at ease in the other's presence. You can let down your hair and be yourself.

9. *If you receive a love letter, or if your lover communicates something meant just for you, are you tempted to share his or her words with others?*

Love is a private bond between two people. It isn't real if one party permits intimate details of a relationship to be made public. This sharing of intimacies may be a bid for prestige in the group, but hardly love.

10. *Do you feel as close (or closer) to God now than you did before you fell in love?*

Connie had never missed a week in church until she met Louie at a church picnic. It bothered her at first that Louie didn't attend church regularly. But he convinced her he got more out of staying home and watching the church service on TV or going backpacking than he did sitting in a pew. "What's wrong with skiing on the Lord's day?" he argued. "There is nothing so inspirational as standing on the top of a mountain and looking out at God's wonderful handiwork."

Little by little Connie began to rationalize away her convictions about worshipping God in His sanctuary on His day. She convinced herself that where she worshipped God was not as important as the fact that she did worship. But when she was with Louie on his weekend outings, they rarely talked about spiritual things. Louie just wasn't interested.

Too many people try to rationalize away their spiritual convictions when their hearts want to pursue a relationship with someone who is spiritually insensitive. Many times you cannot determine whether you have similar spiritual values until you are in a dating relationship. Ask yourself if you are a stronger and better person when you are together. Is the other person seeking truth and a closer relationship with Christ? Are you able to share Christ with each other? If your relationship to Christ deteriorates in a dating relationship, then this relationship is leading you in the wrong direction and should be broken. The chances are high that you will end up unequally yoked together.

If Connie and Louie decide to marry, there is a good chance that Connie's guilt over not being in church would lead her back in that direction, but I doubt if Louie would follow. So instead of enjoying each other's fellowship in church and growing closer together, church would become a barrier in their relationship.

11. Are your ideals and standards the same or higher than before you met each other?

When two people date seriously and begin planning for marriage, the blending of their lives often brings their standards and ideals down to the lowest common denominator. This is not constructive because one partner ends up sacrificing his or her standards. In a positive love relationship, this blending of standards can cause each to become a better person as he or she accepts each other's best.

12. Do you get angry and defensive when someone doesn't approve of this relationship, or doesn't think you are right for each other?

Or can you carefully consider what others are saying and discuss specifics without becoming defensive? True love is not easily angered (1 Corinthians 13:5).

13. Do you seek advice from those whom you admire (teachers, counselors, pastors or parents)?

Or do you know what you want regardless of whatever counsel someone may give, and so don't seek advice and resist it when it's offered?

If it's a lifetime type love, it will weather analysis and grow stronger because of it. And given time, others will affirm that this relationship is a positive one for both individuals. How much happier the wedding will be if you can get married with the blessings of friends and relatives.

14. Is your relationship so involved physically that you tend to ignore subtle irritations, knowing that you would probably feel guilty if this relationship didn't culminate in marriage?

Sex is probably the biggest reason people get married before carefully assessing each other's compatibility. Petting, which leads to sexual arousal, is designed by God to culminate in intercourse. If intense petting is experienced too early in a relationship, judgment is usually biased by feelings. Too often guilt drives a couple to get married prematurely. Just because a sexual mistake has been made doesn't mean that one should rush into a shaky marriage. One mistake is bad enough, and it's certainly better to end a relationship at that point than to compound the mistake with a second by marrying the wrong person. God does forgive.

15. Do you know how each other feels about money, children, role expectations and sex?

True love is practical. It's often the little things that you don't think are important at this point of your relationship that will make or break a marriage. You need to seriously discuss each other's views. You should know each other long enough to observe whether what is said verbally is consistent with one's behavior. For example, Larry said he believed in saving a tenth of his salary. This led Rita to assume that he had a savings account. But weeks later she found he not only didn't have a savings account, but he was also deeply in debt.

Things to talk about in the financial area: What are a person's financial priorities—tithe, family purchases, savings? Who is going to handle the bills and checkbook? How do you feel about separate checking accounts?

In the child-rearing area: Do you want children? When? How many? What types of discipline should be used? What about shared child-rearing responsibilities? Should Mom stay home?

In the role expectation area: How will the household duties be divided? How do you feel about a wife working? Who should make the final decision?

Who handles the finances? Do you consider the wife's career as important as the husband's career?

In the area of sex: What are your expectations of sex in marriage? What about birth control, and what kind is preferable? Is there ever a time to withhold sex from the other?

Romantic love often causes couples to commit themselves to marriage without really getting to know each other. Many couples involved in premarital sex have commented that their communication stopped when sex began. They ended up married without knowing how each other felt about practical day-to-day habits and happenings. Rushing the physical side of a relationship before you really get to know a person can result in a romantic short-term commitment rather than a rational long-term one. Either you're headed down a rocky road for the first few years of marriage, or you'll give up and become another divorce statistic. How much better it is to wait until the illusion of romantic love settles into the real thing before you say, "I do."

❤   ❤   ❤

Something to Think About . . .

Is your relationship still under the illusion of romantic love? Or do you believe you've found true love? Give some examples from your relationship to support your answer. Do you see some areas where you could grow as a couple?

♥ 13 ♥

Making Your Dreams
Come True

Marriage should never just happen. Marriage—
that pivotal point in one's existence after which
everything is affected—should be the most planned-for
experience in your life. The progression of your dating
relationship and the ultimate choice of a marriage
partner will affect your future behavior, your attitudes,
your interests, your friends, your job and your relationship to God. Marriage is a life-changing event; one that
requires a great deal of prayer, soul searching and time.

Marriage should be a dream come true—a dream,
however, that is carefully sifted through the filter of
reality. A realistic dream takes into account the
humanness of each partner, the necessity of forgiveness and reconciliation, the benefits of learning from
painful experiences, and the hard work of saying no to
selfishness and yes to fulfilling each other's needs even
if you don't feel like it or you don't think your mate
deserves it.

Fulfilled dreams don't just happen by chance.
Without a plan, a fairy-tale honeymoon is likely to
vanish with the practical realities of marriage just
about as quickly as Cinderella's coach vanished at the
stroke of midnight.

How do you keep the dream alive when so many couples today have lost the vision of what God intended marriage to be? The answer is to plan for "happily ever after" on a daily basis and to follow that plan throughout your developing relationship.

What Do You Want Out of Marriage?

Now is the time to dream. Be bold. Don't shortchange yourself. Take every wonderful idea that pops into your head, sift it with reality and write your dream here. Dreams can come true.

This dream is your ideal. You may want to modify it as you gain new insights into the realities of what true lifetime love is all about, *but don't give up your dream.* As you move toward a binding marriage commitment, you may expand the scope of your dream to include the hopes and dreams of your loved one. Don't let the skeptics tell you, "It's impossible." The fulfillment you find in marriage may actually exceed your expectations. Anything is possible. But it will never be yours if you don't believe it and don't plan accordingly.

The steps to making this dream a reality aren't difficult to follow. We'll walk through them in this chapter. Believe me, if you follow these guidelines during your dating, courtship and engagement periods, you'll be prepared to make your dream come true.

Keeping Your Dream Alive Through Your Dating Experience

Your dream for living happily ever after starts with *you*. During the dating stage of your life the most important factor that will affect your future happiness has to do with you and the choices you make.

Step 1: Be the kind of person you feel has "great mate" potential.

In other words, be the best person you can possibly be. All of us can find areas in our lives that could be improved. Ask yourself what changes would make you a better person. Evaluate yourself in the following areas and write down your ideas for self-improvement. (If you can't think of any, ask the people who know you best to suggest some ideas.)

Spiritually:

Socially:

Emotionally:

Physically:

Intellectually:

Step 2: Make a list of the characteristics, plus interests, skills and abilities that you would like your marriage partner to have.

1.	11.
2.	12.
3.	13.
4.	14.
5.	15.
6.	16.
7.	17.
8.	18.
9.	19.
10.	20.

Now is the time to brainstorm beyond character traits alone. (That was your assignment in Chapter 3.) Think about interests, skills and abilities.

Remember, you're never going to find your ideal mate in the exact shape and form you have imagined, but this list can help you clarify what you are looking for. And it can form a basis upon which you can evaluate your dates.

Let me give you an example of how you can use this list as a guide without letting it control your life and causing you to become discouraged in your search for a mate. You may be musical; let's say you sing. You put on your "want list" that you'd like to find someone musical who could play the piano or the guitar, or at least sing with you. That's pretty specific. In your search for that person you may find a non-musical someone who has all the *character traits* you feel are important. Now you must consider whether the person really needs to be musical, or is it enough that he or she enjoys the same type of music you do and appreciates your talent? Just how important is musical ability in light of what you consider would bring fulfillment to you in marriage?

Here's some other specifics you may want to include on your list:

Interests	**Skills and Abilities**
camping	artistic
backpacking	mechanical
bird watching	athletic
traveling	gourmet cook
reading	interior decorating
stamp collecting	writer
philosophy	

You get the idea. Hopefully you've started thinking about what is really important to you.

Your list will change based on your dating experience. Dating helps you learn more about yourself and what you really appreciate in others. The more you date, the more your ideas about the type of person you want to spend a lifetime with will gel.

"I want to marry someone who makes me feel comfortable just being me," commented my daughter's friend. Here's what she said about her dating experience. "The first guy I dated was a perfectionist. Whatever it was—his hair, his clothing—it had to be the very best. Even though I was only in the eighth grade, I suddenly became very aware of what I wore, and critical of the way my family did things because I didn't feel they were up to Tony's standards.

"Then came Kurt who was just the opposite. Suddenly I felt it was okay to wear old jeans and sneakers. But Kurt teased me about being a goody-goody because I didn't listen to rock music or go to the movies. While dating Kurt I developed an overwhelming desire to go against the wishes of my parents.

"Then Michael came on the scene. He was not a believing Christian. I didn't know if I should say yes when he first asked me for a date, but he was so polite. When I explained I didn't go to movies, he respected me and said, 'That's okay. I don't particularly like movies anyway. I'd much rather do something so we can talk.' I was beginning to feel more comfortable just being me—and getting a clearer idea of the type of person I wanted to marry.

"Next came a philosopher type, and suddenly I was interested in philosophy. In my freshman year in college I dated a music major. And, if you can believe it, I even considered getting a music minor. Believe me, I'm not that musical.

"Now, I'm just looking for someone who will be so comfortable to be around that I can just be me. And hopefully, if he's the right kind of guy, I'll want to be a better person because of our love, not because I think I need to change in order to be accepted." Then she added with a look of anguish, "Do you think I'll ever find someone like that?"

My answer? If not, don't get married!

Step 3: Date people whom you consider to have marriage potential.

Dating should be fun. Your goal should be to establish many friendships. Don't be so caught up in your pursuit to find the right mate that dating becomes a compulsive, joyless undertaking. Dating is a screening process. Assess your dating friends and evaluate each according to your "want list." If there are some serious flaws in one, move on to other dating relationships. Don't delude yourself into thinking that someone will magically change and become your ideal.

Remember, it is possible to fall in love with the wrong person—and over-exposure usually is the push over that cliff!

Step 4: Don't make a lifetime commitment when overcome with passionate love.

Wait long enough for your rational thinking to catch up with your emotions before cementing your relationship with a marriage license. In other words, make sure your passionate love mellows into true love—the 1 Corinthians 13 type of love—*before* marriage.

Step 5: Move systematically through the bonding process.

Enjoy each gourmet course of bonding to the fullest without rushing toward the dessert of physical intimacy.

Step 6: Throughout your dating, be open to counsel from family, friends and professionals.

Earnestly seek God's will for your life, and don't forget to listen to His Holy Spirit.

Step 7: Don't become engaged unless you are ready for marriage.

The primary function of an engagement is to plan a wedding. If you are just starting your freshman year and don't want to get married until you graduate, hold off on the engagement. If you are currently in debt and want a few bucks in the bank before getting married, wait until you have a sound financial plan before making your intentions public.

Long engagements aren't good. Engagements should only be long enough to plan a wedding and put the final touches on your developing relationship. Talk about marriage, but don't get engaged unless you are absolutely sure this person is the right mate. And even then, as you become more intimate, you may learn things about your partner that hadn't surfaced before that may cause doubts. It's still not too late to back out. You are not yet married. Not until you say, "I do," have you made a binding lifetime commitment to each other.

Step 8: Carefully consider the reasons you are getting married.

You may say it is for love, but it could be for reasons that have very little to do with love. Most people get married for the wrong reasons.

Love, if you define it as the physical desire to be together, is not enough to hold a marriage together. Marriage should occur when the desire to meet the other person's needs becomes greater than the desire to meet your own—and you are ready to commit your life to that purpose. Here are a few of the wrong reasons to get married:

Everybody else is getting married. It's amazing the pressure dating couples experience when their friends start getting married.

Stacy and Jon and two other couples had been dating since their junior year in high school. These six kids had become the closest of friends. Four years later, when the two other couples had gotten married and started spending more of their time with other married couples, Stacy and Jon began to talk of marriage. They knew they had major differences and unresolved conflicts, but marriage just seemed to be the next step in their relationship. It was what others expected of them.

Larry and Nel were in their early thirties, and neither had been married before. They became interested in each other because of their church involvement. The problem was, all their church friends were married. Although not meaning to pressure Larry, his friends did tease him by constantly asking, "Have you asked Nel yet?" Larry and Nel got married because it was the socially acceptable thing to do. Their peers practically demanded their marriage.

Industry makes a wedding look so appealing. One glance through a bride's magazine makes any young woman start to fantasize about how beautiful she will look in her expensive gown and how handsome her tuxedoed groom will be beside her. Add candles, flowers, love songs and those exotic honeymoon hideaways that are advertised, and the thrill of a wedding becomes almost irresistible.

You don't want to disappoint the family. Jessie was a single mother. She knew her children needed a father and Gene was a nice guy. In fact, her entire family thought he was the ideal marriage partner for Jessie. But Jessie never felt the physical attraction to Gene that she thought she should have before marriage. "Don't worry," her friends counseled, "look how the kids love Gene. And look how much Gene loves you."

Jessie went ahead with the wedding, but she continued to harbor doubts and experience feelings of sexual attraction for other men she met. Gene has been a wonderful father to her children, but Jessie still wishes she had waited until she found everything she wanted in a man rather than making a decision based on her children's needs and her family's wishes.

Peer pressure, industry appeal and family expectations are not the only wrong reasons for marriage. Some marry because they are getting older and are afraid they won't find anyone else. Others say, "I do," hoping to get out of a bad home situation. Others simply want independence and they think marriage is their ticket.

But God said we should marry so two people could

become one, and when you are one you love, respect and care for the other person as you would care for yourself. Until your love for each other is totally unselfish, please don't get married.

Keeping the Dream Alive Through Your Engagement

Most couples look back to their engagement as a peak experience in their lives. Here is where romance blossoms. Love may begin in the dating and courtship stages, but now the intensity builds. Someone loves you, and it's no longer a secret. Those nightmarish times of wondering if you would ever "catch" the man or woman of your dreams is past. You are now looking forward to your wedding and to living together for the rest of your lives. You have found security.

But the engagement period is not all candlelight and roses. You have some serious work to do if you are to keep your dream alive during this time.

Step 1: Keep nurturing your relationship by loving actions.

There is nothing like the overwhelming feeling of love—the joy, the fulfillment, the excitement it brings. Affection is a wonderful thing. The desire to be near, to touch and to hold is awesome.

But the strong feelings you have for each other at this moment will only remain and grow if you handle them with care.

Feelings are capricious. They come and go. They fluxuate hourly. They change in a moment with a harsh word or even a "what's the matter with you" kind of sigh.

Some justify their obnoxious behavior by saying they can't control their feelings. Or they let their negative feelings crowd out the positive ones. Slowly love and affection turn to hate and rejection. That's why so many people fall out of love. That's why so many marriages end up in divorce.

Of course, you may not be able to control the initial onset of an emotion, such as fear or anger, but you can control whether you will allow that emotion to continue to affect you.

How do you control your feelings? With your actions. I once read a book titled, *Love Is Something You Do*. I've since forgotten the contents, but I've never forgotten the truth of the title. Love *is* something you do. It's the words of respect you speak, even when you feel resentful. It's the kind things you do for each other, even though you feel like playing dirty. It's going the extra mile, even though you feel taken advantage of.

Don't allow your feelings to dictate your actions. Feelings are too whimsical. If your actions are always actions of love, feelings will follow.

Learn how to love. Learn what makes your beloved happy. Learn how to put your love into words. Learn how to reach out and be a helpmate to each other. During your engagement, learn everything you can about what makes happy, successful, fulfilling marriages, and begin to put these things into practice —whether you feel like it or not. You'll notice something wonderful will begin to happen. Your feelings of love for each other will grow and you'll discover the mountain-tops of love that are out there just waiting to be experienced.

How do I know this works? Because of what Jesus said in John 13:17: "If you know these things, happy are ye if ye do them" (KJV). Never forget that God's formula is knowledge first, actions second and feelings third.

Step 2: Don't gloss over potential problems because you are too busy planning the wedding.

This period in your relationship can be hazardous. If you're not careful, an engagement can sweep you into a marriage before you're really ready. When troublesome things surface, it's tempting to gloss over the problems, knowing that the wedding date is fast approaching.

Just being engaged is not a good reason for marriage. The engagement commitment to marry is conditional. In other words, you and your fiance agree you will get married only if your love for each other continues to grow and you find no reason during your engagement not to get married.

But before you break your engagement, understand that every couple has premarital jitters. Sometime during engagement it's not unusual to have a few doubts about whether you are making the right choice. These feelings are natural. But if you begin to see a number of things in the behavior of the other person that worry you, the wedding date should be postponed until these conflicts can be resolved. Time and physical separation have a way of helping make it clear which way you should ultimately go.

Kent and Marie had a very stormy engagement. Five days before the wedding, Kent was impressed that the wedding shouldn't take place, but after talking to his fiance he decided to go ahead with it. Why? Because he had made an engagement commitment to Marie and didn't feel he should break it because he loved Marie enough not to hurt her.

The result was an even stormier marriage. At one point they even considered suicide as a way out. The only thing that saved them was making a renewed spiritual commitment. Now both Kent and Marie are so committed to the Lord and the spread of the gospel that this common interest holds them together.

Once you have announced your engagement to others, it is extremely difficult to break up without major explanations. When engagement parties have been celebrated, or shower and wedding gifts start to arrive, or the wedding invitations have gone out, some people feel that their doom has been sealed. It's too embarrassing to call things off.

But it's not too late. It's better to be embarrassed and wait until you are sure than to enter marriage with unresolved doubts and end up divorced five years later.

Expense is a big reason weddings aren't called off. Bridal gowns must be ordered four to six months before the wedding. Bridesmaids may already have gone to the expense of buying or making their dresses. Engagement pictures and wedding invitations cost money. You may have gotten non-refundable airline tickets for your honeymoon, or relatives and friends may have already purchased tickets to come to the wedding.

How can you avoid the pitfalls of the engagement hurling you more quickly toward a wedding than you are ready for?

First, don't announce your engagement until you have had premarital counseling. If certain troublesome issues surface during these sessions, you can take the time you need to resolve these differences. Once you find yourself heading toward a wedding date, you won't have that time to solidify your relationship.

And second, during the engagement, don't be afraid to voice your doubts and discuss the possibility of postponing the wedding until things smooth out. It's a lot better to go slow and make sure your relationship is stable than to rush toward a pre-set date and end up spending your first few months or years of marriage going through the adjustments you could have worked through before.

Step 3: Discover each other's hidden secrets.

Now is the time to find out everything about your potential mate. Be concerned if there are hidden secrets or parts of his or her life that are taboo topics. If the road ahead is not yet clear of yesterday's garbage, consider this a warning signal. If your fiance feels that the risk of sharing his or her past is too great, then insist he or she see a counselor. While you don't have to know the specifics, you should talk to the counselor to determine if your fiance's problem could be a potential hazard in marriage.

During the engagement period you'll want to evaluate the minor things you find irritating about each other, and ask yourselves if you want to live with them forever. Don't marry a person for his or her good traits. It's the faults that get under your skin and begin to make you doubt whether you've got the right mate. And don't be surprised if some of these things don't surface until you are well into the engagement period. Some of us become masters at hiding our faults when we want to make a good impression. But marriage isn't an act and usually within a few weeks, we become who we really are. It's certainly better to make this discovery *before* the wedding date.

You also should discover how the person you are marrying reacts in a time of crisis. Many people can mask their real selves when experiencing the good life, but who are they when bad times hit? Crisis has a way of showing a person's real mettle.

What is the characteristic way that conflicts are solved between the two of you—and is this the pattern you will want to follow for the rest of your lives? Let me tell you, if one partner submissively gives in to the other, don't expect this to last much past the honeymoon!

How responsible is this person for his or her own happiness and fulfillment? If your fiance is so wrapped up in you that you become responsible for making him or her happy, that's a pretty heavy burden to take upon yourself. Of those who do, few make it beyond the first year or two.

I've only talked about a few of the significant things to discover during the engagement period. As you grow, you'll discover even more. Don't be afraid to deal with those issues. If you take the time now, on the day those wedding bells ring, you can say without a shadow of a doubt that you have chosen God's ideal for you.

Remember this counsel: "Through wisdom a house is built, and by understanding it is established; by knowledge the rooms are filled with all precious and pleasant riches" (Proverbs 24:3,4). Be wise as you move through these significant years of serious dating, courtship and engagement, and you can have a home where the rooms are filled with all "precious and pleasant riches." That's my dream for you. I hope you will make it your own.

❤ ❤ ❤

Something to Think About . . .

Are you and the one you love on the road to "happily ever after"? Have you set specific goals for your relationship to get you there? If not, why not set aside time in the next few weeks to make some plans for marital bliss? You'll be glad you did.

Letter to a Son Who Is in Love

My Dear Son,

Just yesterday, it seems, you were whispering in my ear, "Mommy, when I grow up, will you marry me?" I giggled, looked surprised and replied, "Of course, but what about Daddy?"

Today you are grown up and in love. What happened to those little boy years? Have I told you everything you need to know to move into your future with a firm step? Have I concentrated so much on shaping the boy in you that I've neglected the man? I wonder, are you ready for love's responsibilities? From my perspective, young love seems so young!

My son, walk carefully through the next few months and years. Love is a beautiful but precarious path. Never before, and never again, will your behavior be so governed by feelings. Sift your feelings carefully. They will undoubtedly whisper things to you that seem right, but in the long run will prove foolish.

God created you with the marvelous capacity to perform sexually, and the one you love probably has only a dim idea about the power she has over you in this area. The way she dresses, her flirting eyes, her caressing touch, her soft voice—any one of these things can make you forget all the sex education classes you've ever taken. So you must be in control. You must be her guide, not her slave. You must set limits and not depend on her alone. You must be mature even though responsible behavior is the last thing you may feel you want.

It's not easy to say "no" when your body, the world and your friends are saying, "Just do it." Our sinful environment has made sleeping together almost as common as a goodnight kiss. You will be tempted to compromise your standards. But by putting this marvelous courtship experience into a lifetime perspective, you'll find that restraint and wisdom now will ensure an abundant and fruitful harvest of love in the future. I'm asking a lot of you, aren't I?

It will help not to place yourself where it's easy to be tempted. Don't spend hours alone in her home or your apartment, even if she wants to. Don't even spend long hours of the night together parked on some mountain lookout. You are the one who must monitor your relationship. She may not always agree with your prudence, but I will guarantee she will respect you for it.

God has made His recommendations of what is appropriate before marriage and what is to be preserved for after the marriage feast. Remember the counsel of Solomon that there is a proper time for everything. He also said, "Can a man hold fire against his chest and not be burned?" (Proverbs 6:27, TLB) In matters that are irreversible, it is always better to be on the conservative side. Learn to deny present pleasures for future benefits.

Your someday-to-be bride is your most precious gift. Don't mar her beauty. Treat her with honor and deep devotion for the gem she is. Don't be tempted to do anything that might cast a shadow on her reputation—or yours. Never ask her to compromise her standards. Speak to her with words that are pure and fit for royalty. Don't let the media pollute your vocabulary of love. A woman becomes as she is treated. Treat your beloved with esteem and she will become your esteemed.

You determine how fast or how slow your relationship will grow. Don't rush her into a lifetime commitment prematurely. Grow together, enjoy each other, laugh, sing, be crazy together, but don't allow the passion you feel now to become so possessive that you prevent each other from becoming everything God wants you to be. Just like a fruit picked green never ripens to its full potential, so it is with a man and a woman.

Have I trained you how to lead and not manipulate? Have I told you how important unconditional acceptance is in a love relationship? Can you accept her just the way she is? Will you love her even if she may not keep herself as trim and attractive as she is now? What if she isn't a good cook and housekeeper? Will you love her just the same? What if she can't have children? Can you live with her through the ups and downs of her monthly cycle? It's so easy to withhold love from a person if she doesn't behave the way you think she should. It's easy for a man to lecture or push his opinions. Can you, in love, hold your tongue—and at the same time express your true feelings? Have you learned this art?

It's your responsibility to guide each date. Do you surprise her with little gifts, a flower or a poem? It's a nice habit to get into before marriage. Do you plan interesting activities so you can get to see each other in different situations? Do you go places with others? It's important to interact with others during this courtship so you can see how you react in different social situations. And do you pray together? A man is to be the spiritual leader of the family. What better place to start than when you are dating. Have you thought of starting each date with a prayer, or maybe ending it that way? That may be even more meaningful than a goodnight kiss—well, it might be!

Encourage her to listen to the counsel of her parents. They have her best interests in mind. Be open to their concerns. Get to know her parents, write to them, ask their advice. I know this will be hard for you. You're probably worried that they won't like you. But someday you'll look back and say, "Wow, that was the best advice my mom ever gave me!"

Son, I can't close without telling you how much I love you. It's a special love we have—mother and son. But now that you are grown, I must be careful not to hold on to you. For your strength as a husband—your whole future happiness—will depend on a complete cutting of the apron-string attachment to me and a complete knotting of the relationship to your bride for a one-flesh, lifelong commitment. Follow God's timetable for your life and you will find true love and joy.

> With special love to my boy,
> Mom

♥ 15 ♥

Letter to a Daughter Who Is in Love

My Precious Daughter,

It's just a few minutes before midnight, but I can't sleep. I feel the need to share some things — things from a mother's heart. Things I haven't said before, or if I have, I think maybe I can improve my thoughts by putting my words on paper.

What does it mean to be a mother? To pray for you and to go for fertility counseling, fearing the experience of motherhood would never be mine. Then the ecstasy of a positive test and the excitement of your first interuterine kick. And finally your birth and the joy of watching you grow more beautiful each day. A bonding so intense, a maternal instinct so strong, that for you nothing was a sacrifice. That's what it means to be a mother.

And now I feel you pulling away. It's God's plan, but how does a mother let go of her prized jewel that she, Daddy and God have fashioned through the years? The mother role I have fulfilled throughout your childhood suddenly has to be redefined. Now I must learn to guide as a friend, and you must, in kindness, let me know when I overstep. But please don't take my concern as meddlesome and prudish. Read on with compassion. Listen to my heart, won't you?

Where should I begin? Maybe with love. You are experiencing love—love for a man—for the very first time. I'm excited for you, happy for you and, yes, concerned. Concerned because I'm afraid you might rush this wonderful experience. Love, like good soup, needs to simmer. Putting it on too hot a burner will ruin it. (That's a cliché—with a flavor of truth!)

I want you to relish each day for what God has in it for you. Don't rush God's timetable. Marriage is for a lifetime, and too many couples plan marriage in the passion of love. Yet when the passion settles—as it will with time—the decisions made will carry on. Will you then have the spiritual, intellectual, emotional and social bonding necessary to hold your relationship together?

If one races through love to a lifelong commitment, some things are missed: relationships with others who will be your social network and support in the future; courses of study that could enrich your life a hundred-fold; intellectual stimulation from long discussions on life issues; cultural experiences—art, music, drama—that make you a well-rounded person. Young adulthood is a time of rapid expansion and change. Don't shortchange your life. I want you to have everything that is coming to you. I want you to have every good thing.

But you will sacrifice all these things if you insist on a passionate race toward marriage. Don't let love control your life, driving you into marriage before you have a chance to become the person you are in the process of becoming. True love is not controlling or manipulative. True love is disciplined. It's a choice. That's why true love is not one's first passionate experience with love (although, in time, it can develop into true love). And that's why true love is so seldom experienced in marriage—and why marriage so often fails.

My precious daughter, you can have everything. *You can.* In God's time, it will all come together like the pieces of a puzzle—if you don't rush biology. Right now everything in your being desires a physical relationship. You must accept these feelings, but not necessarily give in to them. And you must be wise beyond your years not to unnecessarily put yourself in a position where these magnetic feelings move more quickly than reason.

"But Mom," I hear you say, "just because others get in trouble, doesn't mean we will. We really love each other!"

I know you do, Sweetheart, and only you can truly determine the status of your relationship. Just remember, if your relationship causes you to want to isolate yourselves, if you are only happy when you are together, if you aren't drawn closer to your family, friends and God, then your relationship is probably in the passionate stage. In all fairness to each other, you need to give yourselves time to let your love permeate the other areas of your lives.

Let your love relationship be a part of your total growth: intellectually, professionally, spiritually and socially. If not, it's easy to look back some day and blame each other for opportunities missed. If you want the strength of true love that will bind two people in a lifetime commitment, you must not move too quickly. Think about it, won't you?

I know you want to make wise choices. I know you have in the past, so don't think that suddenly I don't trust you. It's just that you've never experienced these strong feelings of love before, and they can give mixed and unhealthy signals. You can't know this unless you've experienced it, and that's why I want to help you so much. Your first choice of a love partner is so important. I just want to give you some input. You need to sift through it and glean what you feel is helpful. I'm like a caution light that says slow down through this significant time, until you are very sure you have God's green light for marriage.

And once your decision is made, Daddy and I will accept it with rejoicing for the love you have found. We just want your relationship to develop in such a way that it will be easy to love your choice of a partner for the rest of your life.

Time has benefits. It gives you a feeling of how well a person wears. Do your personalities mesh? Are your interests similar? Do you respect each other?

Respect may be more important than passion for a lifelong commitment to marriage. Do you respect his initiative? His personal devotional life? His career ambitions? His knowledge? His intellect? His vocabulary? His mannerisms? His friends? His leadership ability? The choices he makes about the use of his time? His interest in current affairs? His interest in developing various talents and skills?

And does he respect you in these areas? Does he inspire you to develop your God-given talents? To aim high? To pursue your calling and mission?

How do others feel about your relationship? Do they think you are right for each other? Do their opinions matter?

Most important, I want you to know that I love you as a part of me. You don't have to do anything to be loved and accepted, and the choices you make will never change that love.

Just because Daddy and I have strong opinions, just because we voice our concerns, just because we say what we feel, doesn't mean that this is correlated in any way with our love for you. You do not have to do exactly what we say in order for our love to continue.

I set you free. You hold your future. God has blessed you with many gifts. How you choose to develop your intellect and abilities, and to apply your skills to life and a profession is entirely your choice. If you just take time to let God's Spirit lead, you'll be everything God intended you to be. And you will experience love to the fullest.

Time tempers emotion with wisdom and good judgment. Don't let biology tamper with time.

You are a special child. You always have been. And we want you to have a special future with a very special man.

Whatever you decide, we want you to know we'll always love you.

Good night, Sweetheart.

> With love ("motherly" love) always,
> Mom

♥ 16 ♥

Letter to
Mom and Dad

Dear Mom and Dad,

I love you and I always will, even though my relationship to you is changing. Don't be hurt if I forget to call, or if my letters no longer tell everything. And if I don't happen to make it home for Christmas, please understand. I'm not trying to hurt you. I'm just trying to get in touch with myself and what's happening inside. I am becoming me—a person separate from my childhood family. A person who is seeking to establish a home and family of my own.

I feel a magnet pulling my heart and allegiance away from you who gave your young lives for my nurture and care, and from the home you provided for me throughout my growing years. I thank you for your love, the sleepless nights and your endless prayers on my behalf which guided me to this point.

I can never repay you. But I can continue to become the person you and God want me to become. However, since I have never gone this way before, my efforts toward becoming my own separate self may be clumsy. Try to understand and don't judge me too harshly. And listen, will you please?

I know you want what is best for my life; therefore,

you are full of advice. I will always respect you for that and will listen to you. But please don't preach. And don't expect me to automatically accept what you say. I need time to consider your opinions, to seek others' counsel, and to finally come to my own conclusions. You have done a good job in training me to think for myself. Trust your work. Trust me.

I know you would like to have a say in who I date and who I will choose for my lifetime marriage partner. I can understand that, after the investment you have made in me, but this must be my choice. I will have to live with this person. I promise I will not make a hasty decision, nor will I make a commitment before we seek premarital counseling to determine our compatibility. I don't want to make a mistake either.

I know that when I fall in love, good sense, at least for a while, is likely to depart. I expect you to say whatever is necessary if you see me in danger. I may not like it, but don't get mad at me if I get mad at you, okay? Somebody needs to keep their cool. I know my rationality will return and I'll be sorry for expressing my angry feelings. And when that happens, please forgive me. I'm still learning.

You have taught me God's commandments and the importance of living a pure, moral life. I want to honor God with my life and do nothing that will cheapen the relationship I want to have with the person I choose to marry.

Thank you for your prayers. I need them. And thank you for your unconditional love. I'll love you always, even when I give my heart and life to another. Thank you for letting me grow away from you, that I might grow stronger and more mature.

> With love always,
> Your adult child

❤ 17 ❤

A Message From Parents

Gloria and Bill Gaither's song, "Some Things We Must Tell the Children," beautifully expresses all the messages parents try to get through to their children, like watching your diet, minding your manners, hanging up your clothes and making your bed. But the years go by so quickly. And although your parents probably found time to teach you how to tie your shoes, ride a bicycle and brush your teeth, I wonder if they took the time to communicate to you the most important message of all—the message that you are loved.

Some of you will say, "Those words aren't from my parents." Parents make mistakes—sometimes tragic mistakes. Some are abusive or neglectful, and some of you are carrying physical and emotional scars that only the Lord can heal. But deep down in the heart of every parent, even though it may be buried under a load of depression, bitterness or hostility, is the desire to give you this message.

You are no longer a child. You are in love, or will soon be. In just a short time, you will be establishing your own family apart from Mom and Dad. Your parents know these are consequential years because they have lived through them. But they can't live your life for you. They must set you free and trust God and you as together you make the most important decision of a lifetime—who you will marry. This choice will shape your future.

Here are your parents' parting words . . .

How can we tell you the things we must tell you
About choosing your lover for life?
To keep yourself pure and seek God's advice
So you won't have a lifetime of strife.

We trust you to live as we've taught you to live,
And we now set you free to decide
Who you choose to date, and whether to wait
For the right one to stand by your side.

But whatever you do, we'll still pray for you,
And we'll pray for the person you choose.
And when you marry your mate, we'll all celebrate.
Just some things we must tell the children.

I hope you're listening.

❤ Appendix ❤

Topics to Discuss Before Marriage

Here is a list of questions that you and the one you love will want to discuss before marriage. The topics are arranged alphabetically and are not in any order of importance. You can use this list throughout your courtship to stimulate conversation, or as a reference to see if there are some topics you have not yet considered. It's important to enter marriage with as much information about your mate as you can possibly obtain so your decision to marry will be guided by common sense and not passion. Discussing these questions now could save you from some unpleasant surprises in the future.

Attitudes

Attitudes About Marriage

Why do you want to get married? Why are you interested in marrying now?

How do you think marriage will affect your life?

What adjustments or changes will you have to make in the way you live?

What goals do you have for your marriage?

What does a lifetime commitment to marriage mean to you?

How do you feel about divorce and remarriage? What does "biblical grounds" for divorce mean to you? Are there any other grounds for divorce that you feel are acceptable? Should couples stay together just because of the children?

What would you do if your mate had an affair? How might this affect your marriage?

What should couples do to promote or maintain a feeling of oneness?

Should you get married if you are in debt? If so, should both husband and wife take equal responsibility for paying off the debt even though one person did not benefit from it?

How do you feel about a wife retaining her maiden name? How about having both husband and wife taking each other's names as their married name?

Attitudes About Your Relationship

What are the three most important reasons you want to marry each other?

What expectations or dreams do you have for each other? Further education? Degrees to be earned? Career advancement? Athletic, musical or artistic achievements? Honors or certificates of achievement? Other?

Thinking ahead ten years, what kind of person do you think your mate will have become? How do you picture your mate twenty-five years from now? What about yourself?

What are three characteristics you feel are most important in order to be a good spouse? Parent? Son- or daughter-in-law? Do you see these in your potential mate?

If you could change something about each other, what would it be? Do you feel comfortable in discussing these things, or do you fear hurting each other's feelings?

Do you feel you will be able to change your mate? How?

When you are together, what makes you most happy? What does the other person do that makes you feel loved?

When you are together, under what conditions do you feel most proud, comfortable, secure, insecure, afraid, embarrassed or frustrated?

In your relationship, what has hurt your feelings or made you unhappy? Why do you feel you reacted like this? Do you see this situation happening again? How do you think you will react if it does happen again?

How do your friends and family view your plans for marriage? How do you wish their views were different?

Is there anything that could happen that would make it difficult for you to continue to love each other? For example, what about becoming fat, bald, impotent, physically handicapped or disfigured, addicted to drugs or alcohol? What would you do if any of these happened?

How do the two of you react when emotionally irritated? Are you satisfied with this behavior in each other? How do you wish it would change? What are the three things that annoy you most? What things easily offend you?

How important do you feel it is to keep each other informed regarding schedules and whereabouts?

How much should you share with a mate about work, other interests, controversial opinions and negative feelings (hurt, jealousy, rejection, guilt, doubt)?

How important is it that you are able to discuss intellectual and emotional issues with each other, like race relations, politics, religion and current affairs? Are you satisfied with the discussions you have had so far in these areas? Are you satisfied with the level of information the other person brings to the conversation? Do you feel your potential mate is over- or under-opinionated? Does this bother you? What was the most recent situation when you wished your potential mate was more open to another opinion rather than defending his or her own?

In a love relationship, what kind of sacrifices should you be willing to make for each other? Should you give up your career if it conflicts with your mate's value system? Would you be willing to give up your job if a move to another location would mean a career advancement for your spouse? What about your educational goals? What about the way you enjoy spending your leisure hours? (If you're a weekend TV football addict and your mate hates it, what should you do? If you love to shop and your mate doesn't, how will you handle it?)

How do you feel when you are separated from each other? How do you think you might react after marriage to long-term separation? How would it affect you if your mate's job required long-distance traveling? Does absence make the heart grow fonder? Why or why not?

What gifts do you enjoy receiving?

How important are the following to your happiness in marriage?

- humor
- love surprises: gifts, special dates, etc.
- appropriate public display of affection
- politeness and manners
- willingness to compromise
- seeking counseling for unresolved problems
- being able to depend on the other
- overlooking faults rather than criticizing
- unconditional acceptance of each other

Other Attitudes That Might Affect a Marriage

How do you feel about authorities who tell you what to do (e.g., the police, the government, the military, parents or grandparents, school or church leaders)?

How do you feel about various professions, such as lawyers, psychologists, doctors, etc.?

What type of a career do you want to have? Do you see yourself being self-employed, in a business partnership, joining a family business, part of a reliable big firm or part of a small hometown company? Do you see yourself as a chief executive officer, a department head, or merely as a capable employee?

How important do you feel further education and/or training is for you to reach your career goals?

Do you have strong opinions about social issues, equal rights, woman's liberation, the welfare system and labor unions?

How do you feel about abortion, euthanasia, prayers in public school, giving out contraceptives in high school clinics, individuals with AIDS serving in health professions, and other hot topics of social concern?

How do you feel about public affection and intimacies before marriage?

How do you feel about signing prenuptial agreements?

Children

Do you want to have children? How soon after marriage? How many? Sex preference? Which first? How many years should be between children?

Is there any reason to question whether you will be able to have children?

How do you feel about adoption? Foster care?

How should children's names be selected? What are your favorite names?

What strong convictions do you have about how children should be raised? What type of discipline should be used and who should administer it? What should you do if you disagree with each other on how to discipline a child?

If you could look ahead fifteen years, what kind of children would you like to have? What would your family look like? What dreams do you have for your children? What special lessons would you want to provide for them? How important is reading, travel, music, art or sports?

What educational aspirations do you have for your children?

What are your feelings about public versus private education? Would you consider home schooling?

What responsibility should children assume to pay for their own education?

What are your feelings about homework? Should parents become involved in school activities?

How do you feel about a woman working during pregnancy? For the first year or two after the baby is born? When the children are preschoolers? School-age? Teenagers? After they have left home?

What are your feelings about day care, babysitters or live-in help? How often should the children be left with others?

How involved do you think you should be with influencing your children's friendships? What ideas do you have about developing positive character traits in your children?

Decision-Making

What is the best way you have found to solve disagreements?

What does the concept of the husband being the head of the household mean to you? What does the idea that a wife is to be submissive mean to you?

How should decisions be made? Who should make the final decisions in the family? Should everything be decided together? What is the role of compromise?

Who should decide the following? (Answer either husband, wife or both. Compare your answers with those of your potential mate.)

- the date and time of the wedding
- the type of ceremony and reception

- the location of the honeymoon and how long it should be
- when and if you should have children
- the number of children
- the selection of the children's names
- the frequency of intercourse
- type of contraception used
- who should initiate lovemaking
- whether counseling is needed for unresolved problems
- who to go to for counseling
- what church to belong to
- how involved the family should be in church activities
- what should be done for family worship times at home
- if the husband should go to school; get a job; change jobs; quit a job
- if the wife should go to school; get a job; change jobs; quit a job
- where to live
- what type of housing is needed
- when to buy a home, a car or other major purchase
- what home to buy
- how to decorate home
- who keeps house in order
- who takes responsibility for home repairs
- who maintains yard and determines landscaping

- whose name the home should be in
- what car to purchase
- whose name the car should be in
- making arrangements for car repairs
- maintaining the car
- how you stand on political issues
- arranging social events and keeping the social calendar
- frequency of going out together
- how weekends and vacations are to be spent
- how much money should be allocated to different items in the budget
- what type of insurance to get
- financial decisions about investments, savings, etc.

Finances

How do you feel about joint checking accounts versus separate accounts? Should all income and resources be pooled, or should his income pay for certain items and her income pay for others?

Who should pay the bills? Who should handle the checking account?

How should decisions be made for small versus large expenditures?

How much insurance do you feel a family needs (life, medical, travel, etc.)?

How do you feel about giving tithes and offerings, or donations to special missions and/or for community needs?

How do you feel about loaning to or borrowing from friends and relatives?

How do you feel about paying cash versus using credit or getting a loan?

What's your opinion about the proper use of credit cards?

How do you feel about going into debt for the following: the purchase of a home, a car, furniture, education, clothing or household conveniences?

How important is it to you to have a savings account? What types of investments would you like to have? Have you thought about setting up a retirement fund or a trust for the children's education?

Have you ever lived within a budget? How successful was your experience? How do you feel about budgeting? How would you feel about going to a financial planner to help establish a practical budget and a financial plan for your family?

How do you feel about get-rich-quick schemes?

How do you feel about multi-level marketing plans?

How do you feel about legalized gambling: the state lottery, slot machines, etc.?

How do you feel about doing things yourself versus hiring services such as house cleaning, gardening, car repair, rug shampoo, window washing, swimming pool care, etc.?

What is your attitude about a wife working outside the home? How do you feel about a wife making more than her husband? Should a family move for a wife's career?

What would you do if you got into financial difficulties?

How do you feel about bankruptcy?

How important is it to have a will? What things would you put in your will?

Parents

What things have you observed in your parents' marriage that you would like to have in your own? What would you definitely not want?

What memories do you have of your childhood?

What family traditions, traits or experiences do you feel might affect your marriage? How?

What kind of a relationship did you have with your mom, dad, grandparents or other family members who were significantly involved in your childhood and teenage years?

Were you adopted? How did this affect you? How do you feel about your birth parents? Would you like to contact them?

How were you disciplined and how did you feel about it?

Did you live in an alcoholic or dysfunctional home? Have you ever gone to counseling because of this? How do you feel this has affected you today? How will it affect your marriage?

Did you ever feel your parents (or some other adult) abused you verbally, physically or sexually? How do you feel about this experience? How do you feel it might affect the way you treat your own children?

How close are you to your parents and family now?

Do you have any hostile or negative feelings about your

family? How do you think these feelings might affect your marriage relationship?

Did you feel you were loved unconditionally or conditionally (only when you were good or did what your parents wanted you to do)? How do you feel this has affected your feelings about yourself and the decisions you have made? How might it affect your marriage?

How involved do you feel you should be in your parents' lives after your marriage? Would living with them ever be a possibility? What about living close to them? How close is too close? How often should you visit or call them? Should you spend weekends or vacations together? What are your parents' expectations in this area?

When your parents can no longer take care of themselves, what arrangements do you feel would be best for them and your family?

What things about each other's parents do you dislike? What do you like?

If your parents were to give three reasons why they wanted your potential mate to join the family, what do you think they would say?

If a parent and your mate disagree, whose side should you take? Do you see any potential in-law problems that could cause conflict in the future?

Should you ever seek parental or in-law advice? When? How would you feel if parents or in-laws were continually giving advice without you asking for it?

Do your parents ever say anything to you that makes you feel guilty or inadequate? How often does this happen? How do you handle these feelings?

Personal Habits

Eating

How do you feel about eating breakfast? A midnight snack? Eating between meals? How important are regular eating times for you?

When do you eat your largest meal?

What does your typical breakfast, lunch and supper consist of?

What foods do you dislike? What are your favorite foods? Do you have food allergies? How do you feel about junk foods, sugar, preservatives, processed foods, white flour, sodas, tea or coffee?

Do you require any special dietary needs, such as sugar free, low fat, low cholesterol or low salt?

Do you enjoy cooking and/or baking? How do you feel about cooking from scratch versus using convenience foods?

Health Habits

How often and how long do you exercise?

What kind of exercise do you enjoy most?

How do you feel about smoking and social drinking?

Do you have any addictive habits: smoking, chewing tobacco, alcohol, drugs, caffeine, coffee, chocolate?

How do you feel about taking over-the-counter drugs or prescription drugs versus using natural remedies?

How willing are you to make lifestyle changes that could improve your health and longevity?

Health History

Are there any medical problems in your family's background that could affect your marriage? Are there any genetic peculiarities or abnormalities in your family? Does there seem to be a history of mental illness or suicides in your family?

What diseases or health problems have members of your family suffered or died from? Have you ever had any of the following: cancer, heart disease, diabetes, allergies, asthma, skin rashes, alcoholism, enuresis (bed wetting), encopresis (bowel soiling), obesity, miscarriage?

At what age do elderly family members tend to die, and from what causes?

Have you ever had contact with someone that makes you worry about the possibility of having contracted a sexually transmitted disease like herpes, gonorrhea or AIDS?

Have you ever required emergency medical care or been hospitalized? Why?

Have you ever suffered from depression or entertained thoughts of suicide?

Have you ever seen a counselor or therapist? Why?

Sleeping

How much sleep do you need every day?

What time do you like to go to bed and wake up?

What do you do if you can't get to sleep?

Do you snore, grind teeth, sleep talk or walk?

What size and type of bed do you prefer now? What about after marriage?

Do you sleep in a room with open windows?

Are you a light or heavy sleeper?

Recreation

How much time should be devoted to leisure or recreational activities?

What do you enjoy doing for leisure? What are your hobbies?

If you had a free day with nothing planned, how would you want to spend it?

What do you enjoy watching on TV? How much time should be spent watching TV daily? Should the TV be on during meals? Do you want to have a TV in your home?

Are there any areas of entertainment that you feel uncomfortable participating in: dancing, card playing, poker or other betting games, operas, rock concerts, movies?

Relationships

Past

What types of friends did you have during your growing years?

What types of activities did you participate in together?

Did you ever get into trouble? Disobey the law? Get arrested?

What is the most painful experience you ever had with a friend? Did you have difficulty making or keeping friends?

When did you start dating? How often? What kind of people were you attracted to? Describe a typical date.

How did you handle breakups? Which one of you broke up? Are you still friends with any of your past boyfriends or girlfriends?

How physically involved did you routinely become with a boy- or girlfriend?

Do you still have dreams about or strong feelings for anyone you used to date?

What was your most serious relationship?

Were you ever engaged or married? Why was the relationship broken? Who broke it? How long did it take your feelings to heal?

Present

How do you feel about each other's current friends? Do some individuals bug you? Why?

Do you resent the amount of time each other spends with his or her friends in relationship to the amount of time spent together?

Future

After marriage, how much time should be devoted to former friends?

How do you feel about having personal friends rather than friends you both can enjoy? How important is it to have mutual friends after your marriage? What can you do to find mutual friends? How will you decide if these friends are good for your relationship?

How would you feel if your mate chose to do something with a personal friend rather than with you? What would you do about it?

Are there certain friends your mate-to-be has now that you wouldn't want him or her to have after the wedding? Why?

Religious Issues

What is your family's religious heritage? Do you want to pass this same heritage down to your children?

How have your parents' religious values and training affected your personal religious attitudes?

Have you had a conversion experience? What difference did it make in your life? Have you always had a close relationship with God? Describe your journey with the Lord during the last five years. How would you evaluate your personal relationship with God? Are you satisfied with it? What changes would you like to make in the future?

How do you feel about various religious issues, such as faith, prayer, baptism, Sabbath observance, righteousness, evangelism, speaking in tongues, hell, etc?

How comfortable do you feel praying, reading the Bible, discussing Bible doctrine or worshipping together with your potential mate?

How do you feel about church membership and attendance? How often should you attend? What services?

How involved would you like to be in a local church? What leadership positions would you enjoy holding?

How do you picture God? Jesus? The Holy Spirit? Do you ever have trouble picturing God as a loving and forgiving God?

Do you feel God calling you to a special mission?

Sexual Values and Expectations

What impression do you have of the sexual fulfillment, or lack of it, your parents found in marriage? What have you noticed in their home or their behavior that makes you feel this way? How do you feel this has affected your own sexual desires and expectations?

How important do you feel sexual fulfillment is to marital fulfillment? How important is it to you to experience intercourse on your honeymoon night? How often do you think a couple should have intercourse? Do you feel sexual fulfillment is dependent on orgasm? Is simultaneous orgasm important? Do you have any thoughts about various positions in intercourse? What have you found to be sexually arousing to you? Are you comfortable with touch?

How do you feel as you think forward to the sexual experience in marriage: fearful, excited, anxious, curious, eager?

Have you had any previous sexual experiences that were unpleasant? How do you feel this will affect your marriage?

What forms of birth control do you prefer? Why?

How do you feel about seeing each other nude? Is there anything about your body that is embarrassing to you?

How do you feel about stimulating your mate's body by hand or tongue? What are your feelings about oral stimulation?

Do you think you will feel comfortable communicating to your mate your sexual desires and telling your mate what is stimulating to you and what is not? Is it difficult for you to talk about personal sexual matters? Do you fear your mate won't understand?

Or do you feel if you make suggestions that you will hurt your mate's feelings? What would make you feel more comfortable talking about these things?

What are your feelings about intercourse during menstrual periods?

What type of an environment do you think you would prefer for lovemaking: music, candles, perfume, incense, soft music? How important is privacy? What time of the day do you think you would prefer?

What will you do if you discover some type of sexual dysfunction in your relationship (e.g., for a man, premature ejaculation or difficulty maintaining an erection; for a woman, painful intercourse or inability to experience a climax)? What should you do if you find that your mate doesn't enjoy sexual intercourse and tries to avoid it? When should you seek sexual therapy? Who would you feel free talking with about sexual problems?

Special Occasions

What kind of family occasions should be celebrated? What about family reunions? How often should they be held?

How do you feel about celebrating Christmas, Easter and other holidays? How should these be celebrated?

Are there any special cultural or family rituals that you want to pass on to your family?

How important are birthdays? Should you exchange gifts? What gifts do you like or dislike: flowers, cologne, practical household things the whole family can use, personal things like an article of clothing?

Thinking Ahead

How do you think you would react to the following situations if you should happen to face them sometime in the future?

- mate sulks, pouts or remains silent for a long period of time
- mate is not willing to share what is obviously bothering him or her
- mate spending time with a former girl- or boyfriend
- mate is not as affectionate as you would like
- mate contracts a major illness or has a disabling accident
- mate doesn't listen
- mate suffers from feelings of low self-worth
- mate loses a job and can't or refuses to get another
- mate hits you in anger
- mate verbally abuses you, saying things that make you feel inferior or worthless
- mate won't take responsibility around the home
- mate criticizes you in public
- mate does something illegal or dishonest
- mate is convicted of a crime and goes to prison
- mate lies to you
- mate quits a prosperous job and goes into own business
- mate's job changes from a day job to a night job
- mate makes foolish purchases and causes the family to go into debt without you knowing

- mate tries to control you with anger, criticism or withdrawal of love
- children come before you planned
- you have two or three more children than expected
- a friend starts making passes at your mate
- you find yourself attracted to another person
- mate is no longer interested in spiritual things or chooses to join a denomination that you feel doesn't believe biblical truth
- mate begins drinking too much or becomes an alcoholic
- mate brings home friends that have a bad influence on your children

Values

What character traits do you enjoy most in others? What things about people do you dislike the most?

List the five most important things in your life.

If you inherited a million dollars, what would you do with it?

If you could spend twenty-four hours with any person, living or dead, who would you choose? Why?

If you had a choice between taking an extra job and earning some extra money or spending that time with your family, what would you choose?

How important is it that you get to the top of the career ladder in your field?

If you could live anywhere in the world, where would it be?

How do you feel about living in the city, suburb or country? How much land would you like to have someday?

Do you enjoy taking care of a yard, having a vegetable garden, or having a backyard swimming pool?

What is your favorite vacation place? What do you like to do on vacation?

What pets would you like to have? How do you feel about indoor versus outdoor pets? What pets would you definitely not want?

Wedding Ceremony

Why is a wedding ceremony important? What should it mean to a couple? What do you want it to mean to you?

What do you want to say in your vows?

How do you want your guests to remember you on your wedding day?

Leader's Guide for *Serious About Love*

Instructions: *Serious About Love* can be used in a thirteen-week seminar/discussion group or for an on-going youth support group. The following are suggested discussion questions to get your group interacting about what they've read.

Session 1: What Do You Want Out of Marriage?

Introduction: Marriage is a pivotal point. In one way or another, everything beyond it will be affected by the one you choose as your mate. Choosing a marriage partner who will stand the test of time is the most important decision you will ever have to make. Yet many people are more serious about checking out the car they want to buy than the person they want to marry. Can you imagine buying a car on feelings alone?

1. How do you feel about the statement: "Marriage is a lifelong commitment to a one-flesh relationship, regardless of personality, handicaps, temperament, money, looks or health. This commitment shouldn't be hard to keep. It shouldn't be work!"

2. What is the difference between putting "effort" into marriage and seeing it as hard "work"?

3. What do you want out of marriage? Here are some possible ideas: romance, intimacy, companionship, a sense of fulfillment, someone to love you, children, security.

4. What should you do before marriage to prevent a relationship from becoming one of convenience?

   a. What about after marriage?

228

b. What might be the first signs of a marriage becoming one of convenience?

c. When the first signs appear, what should you do about it?

5. What should you do before marriage to prevent a devitalized relationship?

a. What about after marriage?

b. What might be the first signs of a devitalized marriage?

c. When the first signs appear, what should you do about it?

6. What should you do before marriage to prevent a dominant/submissive relationship?

a. What about after marriage?

b. What might be the first signs of a dominant/submissive marriage?

c. When the first signs appear, what should you do about it?

7. What should you do before marriage to prevent a conflict-filled relationship?

a. What about after marriage?

b. What might be the first signs of a conflict-filled marriage?

c. When the first signs appear, what should you do about it?

Session 2: Date the Right Mate or Beware of Your Fate

Introduction: It's easy to fall in love. Most people fall in love many times before they are really serious about love—often with individuals who would make very poor marriage partners. Obviously you won't marry everyone you fall in love with, but the chances are quite high that you will promise to love, honor and obey someone you will date in the next few years.

1. Is it possible to be madly in love with the wrong person?

2. Is being in love reason enough to marry?

3. Have you ever heard someone say after the first date or two, "I could never fall in love with him," or "She's not my type" and then end up marrying that person? Why do you think that happens?

4. Is it possible to fall in love with almost anyone? If yes, how does it happen?

5. What's the difference between friendship or casual dating and serious dating?

6. What would you say to a person who continues dating someone just because they are lonely?

7. How can you protect yourself from feeling a relationship is God's will when there are definite indicators that it isn't?

8. What does it mean to be double-bonded?

9. How can you tell when you are dating if one person is overly dependent on the other? What might be some signs?

10. Why is it dangerous to marry your counselor or counselee?

11. How can you know whether the person you are dating has unresolved conflicts from the past?

Session 3: What Are Your Chances of Beating the Odds?

Introduction: Research shows that you will have the best chance of staying married—and being happily married—if you marry someone who is similar to you in age, race, cultural values, education, spirituality and interests. Headstrong love makes a couple think they can beat the odds and find happiness and lifelong fulfillment in marriage regardless of what the research says. But before committing your life to another, prayerfully consider your age, racial, cultural, spiritual and educational compatibility.

1. Do you agree or disagree that opposites attract? Explain your answer.

2. When opposite attraction results in marriage, what is the result?

3. How do you feel about age differences when it comes to marital happiness?

4. How do you feel about racially mixed marriages?

5. How might cultural differences affect the happiness of a marriage?

6. How important is it that a couple have the same spiritual values?

   a. How can you determine whether they do or not?

   b. How important is it that you belong to the same denomination?

7. How might educational differences affect a marriage?

8. What is the ideal length for a courtship? For an engagement?

9. What are the problems that might arise if parents disapprove of the marriage? How can these be dealt with?

10. What if all other advisers think this is a good marriage yet parents still disapprove? What should you do?

Session 4: Qualities of a Great Date

Introduction: List the traits you want to find in a mate, and then divide your list into two categories: (1) Those traits that are *absolutely essential,* and (2) those that would be *nice*—but you could live without them. Discuss why one trait is important for one person but not for another.

1. Why are the following characteristics important to have in a potential mate?

   Trait 1: A happy disposition

   Trait 2: Thoughtfulness

   Trait 3: Not easily angered

Trait 4: Willing to solve problems

Trait 5: Purity

Trait 6: Truthful

Trait 7: Good health habits

Trait 8: Accepts responsibility

Trait 9: Good sense of self-worth

Trait 10: Likes children

Trait 11: A personal relationship with God

Trait 12: Accepts you just the way you are

Trait 13: Willing to grow

Trait 14: Affectionate

2. In your group, what traits were mentioned on individual lists that are not among the fourteen traits listed above?

3. What does the group feel are the three most important traits for a potential mate to have?

4. How important is attractiveness or good looks to a fulfilled marriage?

5. What if looks change during marriage because of illness or an accident? How do you think this might affect your feelings?

6. When might good looks become a negative factor in marriage?

Session 5: How to Be a Great Mate

Introduction: Finding the right person will not necessarily insure marital happiness; being the right mate, however, may. So before going in search of your "Mr. Right" or "Ms. Everything," why don't you take a good look at yourself and ask, "Would I make a great mate?"

1. How essential is marriage to your happiness in life?

2. If you suffer from low self-value, what can you do to increase your self-value and acceptance?

3. Write down the traits about yourself that you feel

pleased about. Write a statement telling yourself how "great" you are in a certain area. Read it to a friend. How did it make you feel when you shared something positive about yourself? Have the other person affirm that positive statement.

4. What is the relationship between accepting yourself and accepting others?

5. Are there things that have happened to you in the past that have caused you to develop traits that may be considered by others as offensive or potentially troublesome? What should you do now to deal with those issues so they will not get in the way of you having a happy marriage?

6. What is gift love? How might this type of love become detrimental to marital happiness? What can you do to overcome perfectionism?

7. How can you determine if you are making wise and mature decisions?

8. How can the development of your spiritual life contribute to marital happiness?

Session 6: Tangling With the Temperaments

Introduction: Read the list of traits in each of the four temperament styles and circle those that describe you. In which area did you circle the most traits? Analyze previous relationships you have had. Did you choose to date people with similar traits as yours, or different?

Sanguine: outgoing, talkative, friendly, optimistic, enthusiastic, cheerful, spontaneous, creative, sincere, curious, sense of humor, child-like, controlled by circumstances, gets angry easily, doesn't hold grudges, life of the party, enjoys being up front, volunteers for jobs, spontaneously touches others, loves to be around others, inspires others, people-oriented

Melancholy: deep thinker, analytical, serious, conscientious, idealistic, artistic, enjoys beautiful things, persistent, orderly, perfectionist, self-sacrificing, economical, enjoys details, easily depressed, pessimistic, avoids attracting attention, suspicious of others, content to stay in background, makes friends cautiously, devoted to others, good listener, easily moved to tears

Choleric: natural leader, delegates work, motivates others, well-organized, confident, dynamic, active, strong-willed, independent, not easily discouraged, goal or product oriented, practical, little need for friends, bossy, is usually right, difficult to see own faults, impatient, unemotional, enjoys controversy, sees the whole picture, excels in emergencies, tends toward being a workaholic

Phlegmatic: easy-going, relaxed, calm, patient, sympathetic, kind, competent, steady, agreeable, avoids conflicts, not easily upset, quiet, keeps emotions to self, good under pressure, has many friends, compassionate, observant, inoffensive, easy to get along with, puts off duties and solutions, dislikes change, takes time to talk and listen

1. What are the strengths and weaknesses of each temperament? Discuss what an individual can do to overcome weaknesses in a particular temperament style. What I've written below will help get you started.

Sanguine:

1. Think of others before yourself.
   - Make others feel special by remembering names and birthdays.
   - Listen to others.

2. Plan and organize your life.
   - Prepare for future events.
   - Pay more attention to details.

3. Carry your fair share of responsibility.
   - Stick to one project until finished.
   - Delegate when appropriate.

Melancholy:

1. Enjoy every day.
   - Be more spontaneous and do things that are pleasurable.
   - Take time to cultivate and enjoy friendships.

2. Cultivate the positive.

- Resist the temptation to gossip.
- Count your blessings and express thanks.

3. Accept yourself (and others) as human.
   - Don't be discouraged with imperfection.
   - Accept others unconditionally.

Choleric:

1. Accept the fact that no one is perfect.
   - Learn to apologize and say, "I'm sorry."
   - Don't pressure others into your "high-performance" standard.

2. Learn to relax.
   - Take time for fun activities and making friends.
   - Plan leisurely activities.

3. Cultivate patience.
   - Don't expect immediate solutions.
   - Encourage others' ideas and choices rather than forcing yours.

Phlegmatic:

1. Pull your fair share.
   - Be observant about what needs to be done.
   - Don't put off doing things.

2. Show motivation and enthusiasm.
   - Try something new.
   - Laugh, smile and show positive emotion.

3. Solve problems when they arise.
   - Learn to talk through problems rather than retreat.
   - Share negative feelings rather than bottle them up.

Session 7: Enjoying the Single Life

Introduction: Read the lyrics (or if you know the tune, sing), "I Wish I Were Single Again." Do you know anyone who has ever said, "I wish I were single again"? Why do you think they said it?

1. How do you feel about being single? If you knew now

that you would never get married, how would that make you feel?

2. What advantages are there in being single?

3. How can you get the most out of your single years?

4. What can you do during your single years to best prepare for marriage?

Session 8: How to Break Up and Remain Friends

Introduction: No one enters a serious dating relationship anticipating a breakup. You expect fun, companionship and romance. When romance is on the rise, there is an exhilarating feeling that nothing could ever go wrong. But it can. The element of romance seldom lasts forever. In that grey area between romantic illusion and true love, breaking up is a real possibility.

1. If you knew a relationship were going to break up after a few months, what would you do to ensure a soft landing after the breakup?

2. Is it possible to prepare for a breakup? What "parachutes" would you hang onto so the breakup would not destroy you or the other person?

3. Is it possible to break up gracefully? How?

4. When someone breaks up with you, what are the five "don'ts" you should remember?

   • Don't

   • Don't

   • Don't

   • Don't

   • Don't

5. Is it possible to break up and still remain friends? If so, do you know anyone who has done this? How did they do it?

Session 9: Symbol of a Lifetime, One-Flesh Commitment

Introduction: Trish and Jon are in love—a true, committed love. And lately they've been feeling some pressure. The hugs are arousing strong responses and the kisses are becoming more intense. They wonder if waiting until marriage for sex is really necessary, or just an old-fashioned concept. After all, they're totally committed to each other. They're mature, intelligent adults. They know all about safe sex and birth control. And they're planning on being married someday.

1. How would you answer the questions young adults like Trish and Jon are asking?

   - What's wrong with sexual intercourse before marriage?

   - Is oral sex outside of marriage permissible?

   - How far can we go before we've crossed the line?

   - How can something be wrong when it makes us feel so good?

2. Why did God create sex?

Session 10: Growing Toward Bonded Intimacy

Introduction: Many sexual relationships are entered into because of the mistaken idea that intimacy can only be achieved by having sex. But true intimacy is not physical—it's psychological. It can be psychological *and* physical, but never just physical. Because sex and intimacy are erroneously equated, too many lonely people jump into bed with strangers and end up dreadfully disillusioned. In their race to what they thought was intimacy, they miss the foundation stages of a relationship that make true intimacy possible.

1. What is bonded intimacy?

2. What are the four relational stages of bonded intimacy?

3. How is friendship dating different from serious dating?

4. What steps within the various stages would you consider most important for the achievement of psychological intimacy?

5. What is the major danger of rebound romances?

6. Is a person's first love experience different from others? If so, how?

Session 11: Courtship Communication

Introduction: It doesn't take long for a lack of communication to destroy a marriage. That's why it's important to learn the principles of good communication during your courtship. *Now* is the time to listen for the feelings behind the words, tune into body language and learn how to say what's on your mind. With a little thought and some training you can smooth out the rough edges of what you say so you can get your message across without causing hard feelings or becoming frustrated.

1. What is the difference between "talking" and "communication"?

2. What is good communication?

3. How do you know when you are really communicating with another individual?

4. Why is it so important to share your feelings?

5. Which of the principles of courtship communication do you find most difficult to achieve?

6. Think of a problem a couple would argue about. First, role play the typical argument. Second, replay the situation using I-messages (Principle 7) and problem solving steps (Principle 8).

Session 12: Discovering the Differences Between Romantic Illusions and True Love

Introduction: How do you feel about the following statement?

Romantic love or infatuation is short-term and has

only the passion. It's a totally absorbing type of love, binding two people in a whirlwind of bliss that makes them oblivious to reason and reality. Romantic love is blind!

1. What kind of problems can you expect when you proceed with a wedding based on romantic love rather than true love?

2. How can you determine the difference between romantic love and true love?

3. What can you do if you discover your relationship is based on romantic love?

4. Does romantic love always become true love if given enough time?

5. If you had a son or daughter who was romantically in love and planning a wedding, what would you do? Can parents do anything to slow down a relationship? Should they?

6. What responsibility do friends have to warn a couple if they feel they are rushing into marriage without the foundation of true love?

Session 13: Making Your Dreams Come True

Introduction: Marriage should be a dream come true, but fulfilled dreams don't just happen by chance. Without a plan, a fairy-tale honeymoon is likely to vanish with the practical realities of marriage just about as quickly as Cinderella's coach vanished at the stroke of midnight.

1. Describe a married couple you know who has a relationship that you'd like to have with your spouse some day. What do you like about their marriage?

2. Fairy tales always end with, "And they lived happily ever after." Is that possible with marriage?

3. Is it possible to have too high expectations of marriage? What is the benefit of having a dream?

4. How do you feel about this statement: "Ideals are like

stars. You may never reach them, but you can set your course by them"?

5. When is it too late to call off the wedding?

6. Divide into four groups. Have each group choose one of the following letters (messages) to read and discuss the following questions: How did the letter make you feel? What was left out? If you were writing a similar message, what would you say?

- Group A: Letter to a Son Who Is in Love (Chapter 14)

- Group B: Letter to a Daughter Who Is in Love (Chapter 15)

- Group C: Letter to Mom and Dad (Chapter 16)

- Group D: A Message From Parents (Chapter 17)